"Finally, a powerful, well-researched bo⟨   ⟩ with and respond to the digital tsunami that's swept over us."

—**Chap Clark**, author of *Hurt 2.0*; senior editor,
YouthWorker Journal

"A cultural wake-up call! *The Digital Invasion* offers timely strategies and practical explanations on how to survive digital damage and put technology in its place."

—**Tim Clinton**, president, American Association
of Christian Counselors; executive director,
Center for Counseling and Family Studies
at Liberty University

"This is a must-read. *The Digital Invasion* offers a wealth of insights in how families can navigate the new digital world that is changing how young people are being influenced and their brains rewired. It challenges us to confront the many myths surrounding digital technology and points us to a healthier way of Internet use."

—**Josh D. McDowell**, author and speaker,
The Unshakable Truth

"This book is a groundbreaking, desperately needed, and long overdue cultural wake-up call that contains invaluable information that you've probably never heard before—information that you need to know for yourself and for those you love and serve. It's not a reactionary 'anti-technology' book but a factual and well-researched resource to help all of us understand the best and worst of our digital world and the profoundly negative impact it can have in actually changing our brains and undermining our relationships. Hart and Frejd don't just expose what is becoming a national health crisis, they also provide practical and biblically consistent ways to deal with it. This unique resource will help you become a more effective parent, teacher, pastor, leader, and friend."

—**Gary J. Oliver**, executive director
of the Center for Relationship Enrichment;
professor of psychology and practical theology,
John Brown University

THE
DIGITAL
INVASION

THE DIGITAL INVASION

How Technology Is Shaping You and Your Relationships

Dr. Archibald D. Hart
and Dr. Sylvia Hart Frejd

BakerBooks

a division of Baker Publishing Group
Grand Rapids, Michigan

Published by Baker Books
a division of Baker Publishing Group
P.O. Box 6287, Grand Rapids, MI 49516-6287
www.bakerbooks.com

Printed in the United States of America

Library of Congress Cataloging-in-Publication Data
Hart, Archibald D.
    The digital invasion : how technology is shaping you and your relationships / Dr. Archibald Hart, Dr. Sylvia Hart Frejd.
        p.   cm.
    Includes bibliographical references.
    ISBN 978-0-8010-1529-8 (pbk.)
    1. Internet—Social aspects. 2. Internet—Moral and ethical aspects. 3. Information technology—Social aspects. 4. Information technology—Moral and ethical aspects. 5. Social media. I. Title.
HM851.H3675 2013
303.48′33—dc23   2013004329

The identity of all persons named in this book has been carefully protected. The names used are fictitious. Major details have also been modified. The authors have tried to conceal any resemblance to actual persons while preserving the gist of the message they want to communicate. The authors love and respect all the clients and acquaintances they have encountered in the past and do not want to break the confidentiality entrusted to them.

13   14   15   16   17   18   19   7   6   5   4   3   2

To my husband, Russ,
I am so thankful for our *"Sweet Love"*
that God has allowed us to share.

To Ashley, Robbie, and Daniel,
you are each a treasure to me and
forever in my heart.
Ek het jou lief.

Sylvia

To my darling wife, Kathleen,
of many years, whom I love more now than
when we met in our late teen years.
The joy we have experienced in our
long journey together
with God as our guide and comforter
knows no equal.

Arch

Contents

i Informational Tip

Assessment

ⓘ Informational Tip

📄 Assessment

ⓘ Informational Tip

📄 Assessment

🛈 Informational Tip

📄 Assessment

Informational Tip

Assessment

Acknowledgments

Dr. Sylvia Hart Frejd

I would like to begin by thanking my Sovereign Lord for calling and anointing me for this project, *thanks be to God!* I am truly grateful to my dad, Dr. Archibald Hart, for giving me this amazing opportunity to join with him. I have loved every minute working with you, Dad, and am truly humbled to have been a part of this assignment. My husband, Russ, who worked tirelessly helping us edit, thank you for being the wind beneath this Songbird's wings—I love you dearly. Ashley, Robbie, and Daniel, my digital natives, I appreciate all your inspiration and even some material for this book, but most of all your love and support of me. Daniel, I am so thankful your dad and I have had these extra years together with you, thanks for all your help in so many ways!

My precious mom, Kathleen Hart, who tirelessly worked with editing, I thank you for your prayers, love, and belief in me; I owe so much to you. My sisters, Dr. Catherine Hart Weber and Dr. Sharon Hart May, who contributed not only their expertise but also their love and support. Barb, I so appreciate you as my sister-in-law and prayer partner; I could not have done this project without your diligent prayers. I am truly grateful! To my friends, thanks for the privilege of doing life together and helping me to find strength for this journey, I love and appreciate each one of you.

Dr. Archibald Hart

I join my daughter Sylvia in thankfulness to our Lord for calling us to this project. Of the thirty books I have authored, I cannot think of one that is as important and timely as this one. My three daughters have encouraged me for several years now to embark on this project, and have provided a wealth of information and research along the way. Sylvia, in particular, has devoted a tremendous amount of her time and talent in research and interviewing key people, and Russ, her husband, contributed enormously in helping us edit the manuscript. And he provided this support at a time in his life when he was facing some serious health issues. I thank you, Russ, for all you contributed.

To my precious wife, Kathleen, I want to especially express my appreciation for her support and prayer. I don't think a day has gone by without her lifting up Sylvia and me to the Lord in prayer.

Lastly, both Sylvia and I are truly grateful to Bob Hosack, our acquisitions editor at Baker, who caught the vision for us to write about our digital invasion. Your support and encouragement to publish this book is much appreciated.

Introduction

What is good about the digital world? Well, you are always reachable. So what is bad about the digital world? You are always reachable! This pretty much summarizes the impact that digital technology with its Internet, smartphones, social networking, and a myriad of other wonderful gadgets brings to our modern world. Ralph Waldo Emerson, reflecting on the changes taking place in the mid-1800s, accurately summarizes our modern dilemma as follows:

> This time, like all times, is a very good one, if we but know what to do with it.

Likewise, our modern digital age can be a very good one, if we can but know what to do with it. That is what this book is all about.

I (Dr. Hart) am writing from the perspective of a clinical psychologist, psychophysiologist, and veteran author who is steeped in research and very familiar with digital technology. Having my daughter, Dr. Sylvia Hart Frejd, join me in this project has one major benefit: she is right at that stage as a parent when all the digital challenges we will be discussing in this book are the very ones she has to deal with daily. She has three children each at a different stage, ranging from mid-adolescence, to late adolescence, to early college. There is hardly an issue we will discuss in this book that she hasn't had to confront herself. I hope that what she has learned "in the trenches" will help us evaluate our strategies before we offer them to you. It will also help us test the digital myths and practices that others are proposing.

As a counselor and spiritual formation and life coach, my daughter, Dr. Frejd, will also help us confront the spiritual challenges that we now face in our digital world. She is deeply involved in church ministry and daily sees the impact of the digital world on people's lives and relationships. She is also certified in Internet Addiction. Together, we hope to present a balanced view of the problems surrounding our use of digital technology. The "invasion," as we have termed it, is happening so speedily that it is almost impossible to keep up with it, let alone predict where we will be five or ten years from now.

This book is a very personal project for me (Dr. Frejd). In preparing to write this book, I have experienced my own technology awakening. Digital technology has affected my family more than I was aware of. I have a teenage son who is very digitally engaged and has fueled my passion for this subject. Over the course of writing this book I have seen him take positive steps toward engaging in real life and limiting his digital life. Spending many months researching technology's effect on our lives and relationships has been an eye-opening experience, and I have had some startling revelations. At times, I wished I could turn the clock back seventeen years, keep the knowledge I have today, and re-parent my children. However, I know that can't happen. My hope is that our experiences and the material we offer in this book will help you and your family to establish appropriate digital boundaries before it is too late, and redeem whatever technology has stolen from you and your family.

But it is not only a teenager's problem. According to the latest Barna Report released a few months ago, the digital age is shaping the parent-child relationship in striking new ways.[1] The shocking revelation from this report is that parents are now spending just as much time in the digital world as their children. That averages about eight hours a day. This discovery is most illuminating as up to now the commonly held belief was that it is only a "young person's problem." The report's very clear conclusion is that it is also a parent's problem. Even more startling is that most families are not getting any form of coaching or teaching on how they and their children can manage their digital technology in a responsible way. Many parents may no longer be good models for their own children and have become as digitally dependent as the younger generation.

Our fervor in writing this book is to share with our readers what we believe is a "faith-based theology" of technology. No doubt, many of our readers are Christian believers. Therefore, like them we believe that God wants us to manage this digital invasion in a responsible way. The misuse of digital technology, as we will show later, can also have a profound impact on our spiritual lives. As believers, we need to be good stewards of the technology that comes from God's creation, and learn what it takes to establish a healthy digital diet.

Throughout the book, we will provide guidance and point the reader to resources that they can use in managing the digital invasion in their lives. We will be as updated as possible in presenting some of the latest research findings in both neuroscience and positive psychology.

However, we also want this book to have a broader application than just in our families. The digital invasion is impacting our educational systems as well as our churches. We trust this book will also be a helpful resource for teachers and educators, pastors, chaplains, counselors, and other Christian leaders who have some influence in our young people's lives. It can also be used as a textbook for college students, since they represent the next generation of parents—the healthier they manage their digital world, the healthier the next generation will be. We offer discussion questions at the end of each chapter to be used in a small group discussion.

We would like to offer a verse of Scripture that serves as a theme for our book. We trust that it will guide your exploration of this critical topic. It comes from the book of Romans:

> Do not be conformed to this [digital] world but be transformed by the renewing of your [unplugged, Christlike] mind. (Rom. 12:2)

So, welcome to this exploration of the digital invasion. We pray that God will give the wisdom and guidance you need to become aware of how the digital world is transforming you and your relationships. Together we will put technology in its place.

Dr. Archibald Hart
Dr. Sylvia Hart Frejd

1

A Brave New World?

Technological progress has merely provided us with more
efficient means for going backwards.

Aldous Huxley

In 1932 Aldous Huxley, a famous writer, published a novel entitled
Brave New World. In it he tried to anticipate the future, portraying a
utopian new world with technology controlling every aspect of it. The
story is set in London in the year 2540, and shows how developments
in reproductive technology and sleep-learning can combine to change
a debauched society. This "future society," according to Huxley, is
an embodiment of the ideals that form the basis of "futurology," or
future studies. In a nutshell, Huxley tried to predict how technology
would control the future world.

It is a fascinating book written in a time when radio had finally
circumnavigated the globe and the automobile was becoming the
main form of transport. It is not very impressive from our modern
technology perspective. Then in 1959, twenty-seven years later, Huxley
wrote a sequel in which he evaluates the accuracy of his predictions.
He entitled it *A Brave New World Revisited*. After carefully evaluating
the changes in technology that had transpired over the intervening
years, Huxley sums up his conclusion in one sentence: "*It has happened faster than I predicted.*"

I (Dr. Hart) find this most intriguing because I must confess that I have been giving a lot of thought to where our modern, digitally driven world is taking us. And I'm not thinking about where we will be five hundred years from now, as Huxley's book was doing, but where we will be in just twenty or thirty years. To some, the explosive growth and powerful influence of our modern cyber world is also taking us by surprise. Even our cyber-scientists are alarmed at its speedy growth. Whereas, the diminutive growth of technology between Huxley's two books did get a boost during World War II with advances in radio communication and the invention of radar, he could never have anticipated the dramatic changes now taking place in our modern world. Nor could he have foreseen how controlling, intrusive, and addictive some of our digital technology would become.

Yes, digital technology has a good side. However, it also has a dark side. Increasing digital overuse is already harming parts of our physical, emotional, relational, and spiritual health. In this book, we want to try to present a balanced perspective on where we are headed. More importantly, we want to offer some clear guidance to parents, educators, pastors, and others about how they can help influence the changes in our modern digital world in a more positive and healthy direction.

Not a Technophobe

Right at the outset let me (Dr. Hart) make an important personal point. Because most experts who question where digital technology is taking us are often accused of being "technophobic" (someone who does not understand anything about digital technology yet is afraid and critical of everything that a computer chip has to offer), I am not—far from it. I offer this short description of my background so you can see where we are coming from as we evaluate our digital world.

I qualified as a civil engineer in South Africa at age twenty-two, younger than most. After a decade of engineering, I felt drawn to "people helping," rather than "bridge building," so I enrolled in a psychology study program at the local university while continuing to work as an engineer. At the end of 1969, I graduated with a PhD in clinical psychology. The statistics for my doctoral dissertation involved more than 2,000 subjects. The university had not yet acquired a computer, so I turned to a friend whose company had recently purchased one and he allowed me to do all my statistical analyses during the evenings. My dissertation became the first PhD study at my university using a computer for analysis. However, it was more complicated than that. No computer programs were yet available for statistics, so I had to teach myself how to write one.

After completing my dissertation and graduating, I spent a year as a visiting scholar at the newly formed Graduate School of Psychology at Fuller Theological Seminary in Pasadena, California. At the end of that year, I was invited to join the faculty as a professor, and quickly plunged myself into psychological research. The seminary did not yet have a computer, so when a "build-it-yourself computer kit" came on the market, I jumped at the opportunity and bought it. The computer I built, named the "Altair," was the same computer that a seventeen-year-old named Bill Gates built. He went on to create the digital giant Microsoft. I reveled in this newfound technology and embraced every aspect of it.

As computers continued to evolve, I stayed close to the technology, teaching myself how to program every new gadget that appeared, even though many of my colleagues saw no future in them.

I went on to become dean of our Graduate School of Psychology and jumped at the opportunity to make us all computer literate. In the early 1980s, a compact, portable desk computer called the "Osborne" came on the market. It was the first commercially successful portable computer, used a single-sided floppy disk drive to store data, and cost a fortune. It offered the first word processor, so I promptly purchased a computer for every faculty member. A few declined my offer, but the rest of us relished our newfound toy. In just a couple of years the Osborne computer was out of date and IBM launched the first "real" personal computer. And the rest is history.

I trust that this brief history shows that I have embraced digital technology from its beginning, and still do. I doubt that I could have achieved much of my success without it. I acquired the first cell phone that came on the market. It was big and cumbersome by today's standards, and you could only get reception in select areas. Within a year, it was out of date. I estimate that over the years I have updated at least twenty-five cell phones. I just had to have the newest and fanciest of any gadget. Recently, I moved to smartphones and now have the latest version of the iPhone, and love it.

Despite my close association with computers, I never dreamed that in my lifetime computer technology would become so invasive in our lives. I expected it to be confined to a narrow group of "elite" users, mostly scientists who could understand the inner workings of a computer. But while I happily embraced the dramatic changes that the digital world has brought, I have slowly come to suspect that it is not all it claims to be.

The Digital Invasion

We chose the title for this book because it is an apt description of how modern digital technology is invading our lives. Daniel Sieberg, an Emmy-nominated and award-winning television science correspondent, expresses it well in his book *The Digital Diet*: "This technology invasion has not been like a nuclear explosion but more like a slow invasion of an ant colony. This technology invasion has been systematic, silent and is destroying many parts of our lives."[1]

If only this invasion had been a nuclear explosion, we would have seen how destructive it could become. But the slow and silent incursion has gone relatively unnoticed. I often remark to my friends that I believe I am living my life at the most significant time in all of history. I would have hated living in an era when computers did not exist! I revel in designing, building, and programming my research gadgets. For a short period in my life, I owned a manufacturing company that built biofeedback instruments. It has always been my passion to stay abreast of this emerging digital world. However, this intimate digital engagement has also allowed me to see the ugly side. First though, let us look on the bright side and acknowledge the good that our digital invasion has to offer.

The Bright Side of Technology

While there is a lot about technology that does, and should, concern us, much is positive and should be embraced. What benefits do computers and the Internet have to offer? Here are just a few:

- We have instant access to a wealth of information anywhere in the world from our computers.
- Social media, like Facebook, have opened up many avenues for social interaction.

- Email is much more speedy and effective than mailing letters.
- You can purchase almost anything from anywhere in the world using online shopping.
- Instant, worldwide communication is available with Facebook, and with video through Skype, Facebook, smartphones, etc. (This is a real boon to families and friends scattered all over the world.)
- Texting provides instant communication and connection in almost any setting.
- For our Christian world, iTunes can give us access to a wide variety of Christian music and sermons.
- The Bible is now accessible in every major language, anywhere in the world.
- Digital books and textbooks are easily accessible for students, and if a student doesn't want to buy the textbook, he or she can get all the information they want from the Internet.

The Not-So-Bright Side

While we now live in remarkable times, we need to accept that the digital world is a double-edged sword. Life for our kids used to be unplugged and carefree. Now it is continuously plugged in to an assortment of digital gadgets that demand attention. Life indoors used to be boring enough that kids went outside and played ball, rode their bicycles, and explored the world around. Now, all the fun is indoors, so why not just sit and enjoy it. Sure, television did intrude somewhat, but it never really dominated our lives to the extent that the digital world does. Today's children are all digital from head to toe, at home and on the go. While television was at home, fixed to the floor and immovable, smartphones are mobile and go wherever you go. They can even go to bed with you and receive and send text messages at three o'clock in the morning. (I, Dr. Hart, have a grandchild in the East who loves sending his grandmother, my wife, text messages in the middle of the night!)

To sum up what we see happening, current parents will be the last generation raised in an unplugged environment. Their children will be the first generation raised in an all-digital, go-go environment. And let us be frank here. We still know very little about what the physical, relational, emotional, and spiritual consequences of extreme exposure to the digital invasion will be over time. We do not want to sound alarmist, but the fact is that our digital world is growing increasingly invasive in our lives. The changes that technology is bringing are so rapid that they are outstripping the human brain's ability to adapt. This is not just our opinion. Dr. Gary Small, a respected researcher and director of the Memory and Aging Research Center at UCLA, has this to say about the changes technology is bringing:

> The current explosion of digital technology not only is changing the way we live and communicate, but is rapidly and profoundly altering our brains. Daily exposure to high technology—computers, smart phones, video games, search engines like Google and Yahoo—stimulates brain cell alteration. . . . Our brains are *evolving* right now at a speed like never before.[2]

Yes, you read him correctly. The speed with which we now process information is changing our brains. This is bound to have many consequences later in life.

This leaves us with the question, Is this "brain change" good or bad? Well, the answer all depends on who you listen to. There are those who uncritically welcome every change our digital world has to offer. They see nothing but good in every aspect of it. On the other hand, there are those who fear the beginning of Armageddon. Thankfully, there are those in the middle who try to maintain a balanced outlook, and whose wisdom we need to heed. Put simply, whether the exploding digital world will have a good or bad outcome will depend on how we manage it.

Without a doubt, no topic is more needful of urgent attention, especially from those who have influence over our children's lives. There is a growing concern that the digital world is stealing a "normal" childhood from our children. Some see it as robbing them of the innocence of childhood. This is a bold statement, but as we will see in the pages to come, many in the scientific, health, and educational world are of this mind. They believe that the creators of this wonderful technology have failed to prepare us for its impact and rapidity of change. Those who have primary responsibility for shaping and molding the vulnerable brains of our children desperately need informed strategies and guidance on how to use this technology in an appropriate and disciplined way.

Digital Natives and Digital Immigrants

There is now a commonly held notion that our world divides into two groups, called *digital natives* and *digital immigrants*. An understanding of this distinction will be helpful as we lay a foundation for the management strategies we will describe later.

The term *digital native* describes those born *after* the advent of digital technology. Obviously, they are the younger generation. This group is also referred to as the "iGeneration" having been born with digital DNA. In contrast, *digital immigrants* are those born *before* the advent of digital technology. They grew up without any digital DNA, and have had to struggle to learn how the digital world functions. In general terms, *digital natives* intuitively speak and breathe the language of computers, while *digital immigrants*, although they may be capable of adapting to technology, don't have any digital DNA to guide them.

There is also an implied belief that digital natives are smarter than digital immigrants. We doubt that this is universally true. The natives may be more current in digital knowledge than many immigrants, but they lack maturity and tend to ignore the hazards of the digital world.

Experts have taken the distinction between the two types a step further. Generally speaking, digital immigrants—those who are new to technology—fall into three major groups. Try to identify where you fit:

1. *Avoiders*: They prefer a lifestyle that leaves them relatively technology-free or with minimal technology. They tend to have telephone landlines, no cell phones, and no email accounts. They do not tweet or Facebook. What is highly illustrative of this group is that they see no value in technology or any of its activities.

2. *Reluctant Adopters*: This group accepts that technology is a part of today's world and try to be a part of it. However, it still feels alien and unintuitive. This group is widely diverse and can be any age. While they may have a basic cell phone, they do not text if they can help it. They may use Google occasionally, but do not have a Facebook account. This group is defined more by its cautious and tentative attitude toward digital technology, rather than by its willingness to use these technologies.

3. *Enthusiastic Adopters*: These digital immigrants have the potential to keep up with the natives. They are at ease in digital situations, and have the capacity and interest in using technology. They may be scientists, programmers, executives,

businesspeople, and others who have embraced technology enthusiastically, and immerse themselves in the Internet culture. This group tends to see only the good in technology (perhaps too blindly) and do their best to make maximum use of it.

Like digital immigrants, digital natives are also not created equal. They are also a diverse group in terms of their attitudes and usage of digital technologies and fall into the following three groups:

1. *Avoiders*: Yes, there are some young people, even though they were born digital, who do not feel an affinity for digital technologies. Unlike most of their peers, they are not enamored with Facebook, texting, or mobile technologies. Members of this group may use a regular cell phone, but little else. As you can expect, they are a small group who avoid the digital world and may feel ostracized, and since they are young, experience some bullying or teasing.

2. *Minimalists*: They realize that digital technology is here to stay and embrace it as a part of today's world, but they limit their engagement and use it only when they perceive it is necessary. Minimalists Google for information only if they have to. While they may have a Facebook account, they check it only once a day or every couple of days. They will ask directions to a friend's house instead of simply getting the address and looking it up on Google maps. If absolutely necessary, they will use Skype or a GPS system, but they are not eager to do so.

3. *Enthusiastic Participants*: They constitute the majority of youth today and make up most of the digital natives. They enjoy and thrive on technology and its gadgets. They always want the absolute latest smartphone even if the latest model has only a miniscule change (which makes for good sales). They constantly interact through Facebook, Twitter, and texting. They are online in some capacity (YouTube, watching television shows or movies online, Facebook, surfing, etc.) all day long or as much as possible. When they want to know something—such as a language translation, directions to a party, the spelling of a word, or even the answer to an exam question, they turn to Google. This group thrives on instant communication, even if it means severe sleep deprivation.

Younger members of the Enthusiastic group prefer texting to emailing. Generally speaking, the younger generation is becoming less and less prepared to write in a professional manner. This sets them up for digital divide clashes at home, school, the workplace, and any other situation where digital immigrants set the tone. Enthusiastic participants include (but are not limited to) online gamers and those first in line to buy the latest smartphone. They find technology exhilarating.

Conflicts between digital natives and immigrants are now a fact of life. There will come a day when all humans will be natives and the conflict will diminish, but until then, parents and children will be at odds with one another. Bureaucracy, paperwork, and formalities will make little sense to the natives, and instant access online to teachers, peers, and parents will be the norm.

An understanding of the basic differences between digital immigrants and natives can help alleviate the tension between them and lay the foundation for an overall healthier engagement of all groups. For those immigrants who are not well versed in digital language or Internet terminology, we offer a "Social Media Glossary" in appendix A for you to review.

The Digital World and Our Spirituality

Let us not forget that the digital invasion will also influence our spiritual lives. As Christian believers, we need to pay careful attention to the astonishing changes that our technologically driven world is having on our spirituality. For example, researchers are warning that the ability to "contemplate" or "meditate" declines in those who over-engage the digital world. We already see this in many young people today. They prefer action-oriented spiritual activity to reflective or meditational spirituality. Any call to meditate or reflect on something spiritual falls flat. Rather than just listen to sermons, they prefer videos or skits. "Worship," as many digital immigrants understand it, is not what the natives prefer.

Clearly, this will have an effect on their ability to spend any significant time in prayer, let alone reflect on Scripture or pay attention to a deep sermon. In addition, these consequences must inevitably affect their spiritual practices as well.

Is there widespread evidence of this change taking place in our churches? We believe there is. Several pastors we interviewed reported

that increasing numbers of their congregants were distracted by the
texting going on during worship, and especially during the sermon. I
(Dr. Frejd) recently interviewed several pastors to get their opinion about
the impact of the digital world on their ministry. One is a college pastor
who has close contact with college age youth. This is what he had to say:

> I see young people losing the interpersonal skills it takes to function
> in relationships, in a family, and in the church. My concern is how this
> lack of communication will affect their marriages and the way they
> parent. This digitally dependent generation is not able to take in a lot
> of information and get deep. They aren't reading books and it is chang-
> ing their learning style. They have a high need for distraction, so my
> teaching style has to adapt. As Andy Stanley has said, I have to teach
> less for more. I believe that parents should not live in a cocoon. Don't
> disengage, but get involved in their child's digital life. I believe the most
> damaging effect of the digital world to be the parent's own dependence
> on digital media because it will become their child's dependence.

I (Dr. Hart) spoke at a regional pastors' conference recently. Between my two presentations, the leader asked all pastors to take out
their smartphones, access an app, and vote on a particular issue. Up
until then all cell phones were neatly pocketed and out of sight. After
being encouraged to use it, it remained accessible and ready for action. While I was presenting in the next section, I noticed that many
of the pastors continued to text each other. It was obvious that they
were continuing their discussion of the topic on which they had just
voted. It was most distracting. As a professor, I am quite accustomed
to this "hidden" activity on smartphones or laptop computers by students, but I found it most impolite that a group of pastors should be
so insensitive to a conference presenter. Obviously, our smartphones
are capable of doing many wonderful things. Surely, there comes a
time when simple etiquette requires that it be set aside. I am sure this
is what they expect from their members whenever they preach.

Our digital world is more invasive in our church life than just this.
The pastor of a large church who recently attended a seminar I (Dr.
Hart) was teaching expressed deep frustration over the intrusion of
smartphones in his church's worship time. This is what he wrote in
a subsequent letter to me:

> When you spoke about the problems we face in our digital society I felt
> jerked out of my artificial church world. I realized how far from reality

our congregations have gone and how much of my time and energy is poured into problems that, if rectified, will make little positive impact on anyone's life! I hadn't realized the level to which engagement with the digital world was making it difficult for my people to just think, let alone worship. Nor had I realized how much it contributes to the "dumbing down" of our students, making it more difficult for them to problem solve, meditate, contemplate and even connect ideas together. It made me think of the ways I have allowed technology to encroach on my own quiet times with the Lord in the morning, or my being present with people in conversations. My cell phone vibrates, or my computer dingles to tell me that I have email. I am distracted from being fully present with my people, even at meetings. It is both rude and debilitating for me and the conversation or presentation that is going on in my distracted presence.

There are scores of pastors who feel this way. We encounter them often. I hope that as we work our way through the broader challenges that our digital world offers, pastors will be able to set clearer boundaries, for themselves and their congregations.

Parents and Educators CAN Make a Difference

In preparing to write this book, we wanted to be as well informed as possible about the challenges parents were already facing from the digital invasion. So we talked with many parents on both sides of the continent about their struggle with their children's exposure to the bad side of modern technology, and tried to assess what they needed to know in order to rein in their family's overuse of digital technology.

Our findings from this informal research were most illuminating and confirmed our worst fear: digital engagement seems to be breaking down their sense of unity as a family. Many parents confessed that they were as hooked on their computers and cell phones as their kids. Many teenagers reported that they often sit together as a family in their "family" room, but hardly speak to each other because they are engaged elsewhere on their cell phones. Dads admitted that they were as addicted to certain Internet activities as their kids. Moms sit texting while nursing their babies, impacting the face-to-face bond of mother and child. Both are preoccupied with his or her digital gadgets, and engaging this way separates them into different worlds. Texted conversations may go back and forth between family members while sitting together, but hardly a word is spoken.

Many of the parents also acknowledged that they had no sense of the seriousness of the emotional and physical challenges that the digital world had to offer. We have a friend who is currently suffering from a severe vision problem. At first, she experienced severe zigzagging, and then it became a flashing variation of colors. Her eye specialist told her that extreme use of her computer and smartphone was most likely to blame and instructed her to cut back on their usage drastically. She had also developed a severe carpal tunnel syndrome, where extreme pressure on a nerve in the wrist that supplies feeling and movement to parts of the hand can develop from keyboard overuse. She also developed the classical symptoms of numbness, tingling, weakness, or muscle damage in the hand and fingers. All of these problems are related to excessive computer use.

It was also very clear from our informal survey that adults had minimal understanding of what was good or bad about their, or their children's, cyber-world engagement. They just assumed that because "everyone else was doing it" it must be OK for them to do the same. They certainly had no clear plan of action for preventing the negative consequences of digital engagement. They all expressed a strong need to learn more about how to lead their families into a healthier, disciplined engagement of technology, so that they could all reap the positive benefits it has to offer while ensuring that the negatives are kept to a minimum.

In addition, parents also struggle to deal with the resistance they encounter from the digital natives. It comes across as meddling in their children's world. A schoolteacher and father of a fourteen-year-old son was honest, when in his comments at the end of a seminar we were teaching, he described a typical dilemma facing many parents when they try to rein in their children's digital usage.

He explained that his teenage son spends a lot of time texting his buddies. Like so many, he does it mostly in the late-night hours when the rest of the family is asleep. The son was failing badly at school, mostly because he was not getting proper sleep. His teachers complained to the parents that he was falling asleep during class (more so than other students) and even went so far as to suggest that the boy might be suffering from ADD (Attention Deficit Disorder). It just so happens that recent research confirms that sleep deprivation in children can cause a "pseudo" form of ADD. The father was quite distraught as he expressed his frustration. Then he explained the quandary he was in:

> I know I should take my son's cell phone away when he goes to bed. But if I take it away my fear is that he won't be able to respond to the text messages going between his other friends, and they will only ostracize him. Since every other kid is doing it, I'm reluctant to deprive him of it. He will just be treated like some oddball. I suppose I feel that good friendships are just as important to a teenager as good grades. I have no idea what I should do.

We understand this father's dilemma. This is the reason why parents need training in when and how to set digital limits. They need counsel in how to take a courageous, disciplinary stand so that the final outcome will most benefit their children.

We will address these issues and offer practical help to struggling and perplexed parents. Our plea here is that parents don't surrender to the status quo, but take the time to educate themselves about the growing hazards of the cyber world, and find the balance that benefits their children the most.

What We Can Do about It

Protecting your children has to be your highest priority. We cannot stress strongly enough that the challenges we face have already begun to take their toll in both the physical and emotional health of our children.

Of course, the solutions we offer will limit the amount of "excitement" in your child's life. There will be pushback. Parents will have to rediscover what an important word "no" is, and conjure up the courage to say it, often. Parents need to know when "Enough is enough," as far as digital usage goes. They will have to set a time in the evening when the Wi-Fi system feeding the whole family gets unplugged, or when all cell phones should be placed in a conspicuous basket and left there until the next morning—turned off, of course. Internet video gaming and Facebook will need to be deferred until all homework and chores are done.

If your children complain that they "are bored," help them remedy their boredom by playing an outdoor game with them. Yes, we mean with them! Years later you will hear them tell your grandchildren about the games they used to play with you on the lawn or in the park, and you will be glad you did. Alternatively, take them for walks, and find a non-cyber hobby that you can all engage in. Have them walk the dog, read a magazine or a book (yes, an ebook would be OK), or help them learn a musical instrument or a foreign language. If they claim that it is "not fair" or that "everyone else is doing it," then remind them that *you* are the parent responsible for how they turn out, not "everyone else's" parent.

Fortunately, the scientific world is waking up to the seriousness of the challenges that cyber-technology presents and is beginning to come up with helpful strategies. What waits to be seen is whether moms and dads (and others involved in raising our kids) will wake up to the threats our digital world poses and take positive action. We believe that there ARE strategies that parents and teachers can use to counter the consequences of Internet and digital-technology abuse. The solutions, simple as they may seem, may be difficult for many parents to enforce, but *every* parent needs to wake up to the seriousness of the challenge facing them.

It is our hope that this book will provide you, the reader, with the knowledge, wisdom, determination, courage, and tools needed to turn a potential disaster into a great blessing for all. We don't want to limit this book to just protecting our children from the obvious, more serious risks of the digital world, such as cyberbullying or sexual harassment, but from the more subtle and common risks that hide behind the "well, everyone else is doing it" excuse. We will focus on all who are at risk by the digital invasion—both digital natives and digital immigrants.

There is growing evidence that our cyber world can have a negative effect on every aspect of our lives, including our physical and mental health, our marriages, occupational success, and much more. This next generation is at great risk of not being able to cultivate deep and intimate relationships. We hope to provide focused resources in all these areas to help guide you through the challenges you face in our "Not-So-Brave New World." We trust that our approach is balanced and realistic.

Yes, the suggestions and recommendations we will offer will take some of your time and demand a cooperative effort by both parents and all who come into contact with our children. It will leave you praying a lot for the courage and wisdom to make even the smallest progress, *but it must be done now*. Digital natives may know more about today's technology, but digital immigrants know more about real life.

Discussion Questions

1. Are you a *digital immigrant* or a *digital native*? Which group below do you fall into?
   - *digital immigrant*—avoider, reluctant adopter, or enthusiastic adopter
   - *digital native*—avoider, minimalist, or enthusiastic participant

2. How do you think technology is stealing a "normal" childhood from your children? Have you had any personal experience with this? Share your story.

3. Late in this chapter we tell the story of a father facing the dilemma of trying to rein in his teenage son who spends a lot of time texting his buddies. He feared that his son would be ostracized. Can you relate to this dilemma? How?

4. What are some of the positive effects that technology has brought into your life?

5. Why do you believe there is a sense of urgency in turning the phenomenal digital world into a helpful, nondestructive, life-building tool?

6. After reading what's been covered in this chapter, what initial steps would you say are necessary to manage how digital technology is affecting you and your family?

2

Awaken to Your Relationship with Technology

Awaken—to arouse, to waken from sleep or a similar state, to get up.

Technology promises to let us do anything from anywhere with anyone. But it also drains us as we try to do everything everywhere. We begin to feel overwhelmed and depleted by the lives technology makes possible. We may be free to work from anywhere, but we are also prone to being lonely everywhere.

Sherry Turkle,
professor of the Social Studies of Science, MIT

"Mark, can you give Allie a bath tonight? I am really tired," Sarah asked her husband after they finished dinner. "Sure," Mark replied, and headed off to the bathtub with Allie. But the whole time his little daughter was in the bathtub, he was playing games on his smartphone. Later that evening, as Mark lay in bed reflecting back on his time with Allie in the bathtub, he had a revelation. He turned to Sarah. "Honey, I've just realized I was focused on my smartphone the whole time Allie was in the bathtub. That isn't what a father should be doing during such a special time. These are moments she'll remember all her life and I was just wasting time with my phone. It really concerns me that my compulsion to play games on my smartphone is greater than my desire to spend time with Allie." That night was a wake-up call for Mark about his relationship with technology. He decided that he would make some changes.

Like Mark, we all need to pay attention to our relationship with technology. This chapter is a clarion call for all of us to *wake up* and assess what our relationship with technology might be doing in our lives. There is no doubt that this digital world has taken over and is shaping our real life. Take a moment right now and reflect on how modern technology is changing *your* life. You might even want to write down some insights. Would you say that you are receiving a lot more enjoyment from your digital gadgets than your real-life connections? If so, then why? Does a typical day in your life look like this: You wake up with your alarm screaming at you, then you check your email, check Facebook, check Twitter, check your email again. You receive a text and reply immediately to said text. When you get home from work, it starts all over again as you repeat this ritual until bedtime (some all night long!).

Where Has All the Time Gone?

It's hardly news that young adults are the most digitally connected, but now Nielsen has come up with a new name for this group based on their common behaviors: Generation C. The C stands for "connected," and the group comprises Americans between eighteen and thirty-four who are defined by their digital connectivity; they consume media, socialize, and share experiences through devices more than other age group.[1] It is not just the eighteen- to thirty-four-year-olds who want to be connected constantly. We all expect to be reachable all the time.

It is not surprising to learn that Internet-connected mobile devices have also aided the growth in Internet use as every smartphone has Internet access. By 2015, an estimated 82 percent of households will have Internet connections. Soon everyone will be on the web in one way or another.

Our smartphones and iPads are just a click away from the latest news byte, bit of gossip, and anyone wanting to communicate with us. Unfortunately, this sometimes includes total strangers who believe they have the right to intrude anytime it suits them. That flashing notification on your phone for an incoming email, a text message, or a Facebook post becomes an arousal trigger that can invade your life at any given moment. This affects not only you but also your loved ones who need your attention. It becomes a struggle to hold a conversation with friends without our eyes darting back and forth to check our phones for an incoming message.

Most of the time we are not aware of how intrusive this perpetual and easy communication access has become, or how much of our time it demands. It certainly does bring us easier and faster communication, and for this we are very thankful. However, we also need to be aware of how our over-engagement of the digital world can undermine our lives. It is doubtful if this over-engagement draws us closer together in our most meaningful relationships.

Many people are now saying, "My smartphone is an extension of myself. How could I survive without it?" *Nomophobia*, "no-mobile-phone phobia, is on the rise. It is the newest digital disorder named for the fear of being separated from your cell phone. Without a doubt, our smartphones and other digital products have become an integral part of our lives, in some cases to the extent that we cannot survive without them. Part of the "awakening" we are pleading for here arises because digital products do not just attach themselves to our lives. They take over our lives. The risk of developing an addictive bond to our smartphone or some Internet activity is becoming increasingly and unavoidably compulsory if we continue on the path we are on. Our digital toys and tools may not have been intentionally designed to create such addictions, but nevertheless, they have become one of the greatest addictive challenges we have ever had to face. For most of us, it's not a matter of *if* we are addicted but *how bad* do we have it.

We All Have a Relationship with Technology

What is your relationship with the digital gadgets that surround you every day? Most of the time, our gadgets are waiting in the shadows ready to demand our immediate attention. They have also quietly changed our attitudes. Take email for example. Hardly a day goes by without someone expecting a quick response from me to an email. Why else do we have emails if one cannot expect an immediate reply?

Our digital gadgets have the ability to fragment our focus. They can be intrusive in whatever task we are performing. My (Dr. Hart's) dear wife keeps in close contact with all our grandchildren as well as many of the pastor's wives she has mentored over the years. She also loves to garden. But I have noticed that she usually goes into the garden with her cell phone. The reason is obvious: she wants to be available when they call. She sees it as part of her ministry. We carry our cell phones into every activity, including those that require careful attention, and it is as if we have given our mobile phones the privilege of intrusion, whereas no one else has that same privilege.

Our digital gadgets are not only privileged intruders, they provide a subtle form of excitement and arousal that overloads our brain's pleasure system, and often lead to obsessive habits and emotional dependency. We came across a blog recently, where a man was explaining his relationship to his digital world:

> In real life people make demands of me. It takes energy to connect and talk and work through conflict and resolve issues. My smartphone makes no such demands on me. It offers pleasure 24/7. My brain craves the instant gratification and pleasures the text or email offers. The more I look at it and use it the more dependent I become on it.

A man shared the following story with me (Dr. Frejd). Last week he went to work without his smartphone. He was in a hurry and accidentally left it on the breakfast table. The "receive call" setting on his phone was on vibrate. All that day, without his phone, he experienced phantom vibrations. He would reach for his phone believing there was an incoming call, only to find that there was no phone there. He had heard about how amputees could feel phantom pain in a missing limb, but never realized it could happen to him with a phone in a pocket. I have shared this story with other people and many report experiencing the same phenomenon: the vibration on their skin from their phone becomes a phantom vibration over time. We gave this disorder a name— it's "Phantom Cell phone Vibration Disorder" or PCVD for short!

But our concern is not just about bothersome phantom vibrations. The bigger issue is where our culture is headed in regard to our relationship with technology at large. It is reshaping our lives, but we are not paying a lot of attention to the change. So let's take a step back and briefly reflect on where we are headed. If you were to put this book down right now, drive over to your local shopping mall, and take a stroll (with your smartphone tucked safely in your pocket or purse, of course) you would observe people talking, texting, messaging, Googling, accessing Facebook, and even playing games or listening to music on their smartphones. We are becoming a generation beholden to our mobile digital gadgets. Smartphones are taking over. A new study shows that more than one billion people are using a smartphone. It is believed that by the year 2015 there will be over two billion smartphone users.[2]

The 2011 Barna family report reveals that many of us are spending as much as eight hours a day in the digital world.[3] According to this report, the digital age is shaping the parent-child relationships in striking new ways. The following are some of the findings from the report that can help us as we reflect on, and try to come to terms with, our relationship with technology:

1. Parents are just as dependent on technology as are their teens and tweens. Parents are using technology and media to nearly the same degree as their 11- to 17-year-olds. Younger parents, the digital natives in their 30s and 40s, are even more dependent on technology.

2. Most family members feel that technology has been a positive influence on their families and welcome technology and media with open arms rather than with caution.

3. Very few adults or youth take substantial breaks from technology. This confirms that Americans are increasingly becoming dependent, if not addicted, to technology. Only 10 percent of parents and 6 percent of teenagers say they try to take one day a week off from their digital usage. The question that arises is whether families are in control of their technology or being controlled by it.

4. Families experience conflict about technology, but not in predictable ways. The research states that technology seems to amplify the relational patterns and problems that are already in place. Families that have healthy and frequent conversations find technology aiding that process, while families without such healthy interactions find that technology exacerbates the isolation of its members.

5. Our younger people feel that there is a double standard with digital rules. Their parents are telling them to get off the

computer or to not text at the dinner table, but don't do so themselves. They are not modeling good digital boundaries.

6. Few families have experienced or expect to experience churches addressing technology. Most parents and children have not heard any kind of teaching in a church, religious setting, or public forum (like a school) about how families can best use media, entertainment, and technology, and are not getting any coaching or assistance when it comes to healthy integration of technology into their family life.[4]

There is no doubt that we have formed a strong attachment to our digital gadgets. That laptop or smartphone you have is not inherently evil, but the value you place on it will determine whether it serves you or you serve it.

More Socially Connected, but More Disconnected

We also need to awaken to how our digital world is changing our social connections. The growing belief that connecting socially over the Internet using a computer or smartphone is as good as, and possibly even better than, old-fashioned face-to-face communications also needs to be addressed. *"The more we connect the better"* is a great motto, but *how* we connect in modern times needs close scrutiny to ensure that we are on the right track with our pursuit of more social connections.

As a culture, it is assumed that we are more "connected" today than we have ever been in history, but there is evidence to suggest that we are actually more disconnected than ever before. How we define "connection" is very important. We are in contact with many people on the subway train, but not really connected with anyone. Also, connecting with a friend using Skype, for example, where we see our friend on a computer screen is NOT the same as connecting with a friend over a cup of coffee. Ask a dating couple whether they could effectively "date" if the only way they connect was using Skype on a computer screen, and they will tell you "no way"! In person we connect not just with what we see, but through our touching and other senses as well. These senses, experts tell us, need to be a part of a "real" social encounter.

There is a place for Skype connections. I (Dr. Hart) am always asking my children and grandchildren to Skype me or do a FaceTime chat on their iPhone. Of course, the visual connection helps when you already know someone very well, but if you do not, it doesn't really add anything to the relationship. A video connection via the Internet, therefore, is only a meaningful connection if it supplements the personal contacts previously established face-to-face. This leads us to the obvious conclusion that Skype, Facebook, smartphones, and all the other social networking applications we have created are meaningful up to a point, but do not offer, in and of themselves, real intimate social connections. As social augmenters, they are exceptional and very convenient. We can stay in touch with family members who live on the other side of the country. But, and this is a big "but," the more we come to depend on the social connectedness offered by our digital world, the more intentional we must be in creating and sustaining *real* connectedness.

The issue of digitally mediated social media presents another problem for us as Christian believers. We may rue the day when, for instance, church worship will not be the physical gathering of a group of people, but an online gathering where you join in worship with others, from your own living room. Why, you don't even have to stand to sing a hymn or worship song, just stay put on the couch. Many churches are offering Internet worship services, and while they may be effective in recruiting many to attend a live church service, it can also encourage others to stay at home and worship.

But even if you supersize your television and the church offers the service in 3D, it will not be the same as joining physically with other worshipers. Perhaps we are too old-fashioned. But why stop here? Let's take our postulate a step further. In the future, we will probably not all worship at the same time anyway. We will choose the time of day to fit our busy schedule, and just replay our selected worship service at a more convenient time. And you can do it all by yourself. Who needs people?

Despite the obvious shortcomings of our modern digital social connections, they have become a worldwide phenomenon with a following of over 550 million people—and are growing by leaps and bounds. What accounts for this dramatic growth? Dr. Nicole M. Radziwill, in her book *Disconnected*, writes:

> I've heard that admitting you *have* a problem is the first step towards *fixing* a problem. This is my confession. I am a social media addict. I did some data collection the other day and discovered just how bad my problem is. 1) I was checking Twitter (on average) every 8 minutes

while awake. 2) I was checking Twitter nearly every 48 minutes while asleep. Since I sleep for eight hours a night that translates into 10 Twitter checks *while asleep* and 120 checks a day *while awake*. . . . I was checking [my smartphone] about once every 2.5 minutes while awake . . . not counting the times I wake up in the middle of the night, which would put me over 400.[5]

Dr. Radziwill is not alone in questioning her social media abuse. Simply Googling "technology addiction" yields over 66 million results. So, how did we get to this place with technology? It appears that as a society we have become more disconnected and impersonal, and in many ways we could say "faceless." Facebook and smartphones came along and filled the need for more connections with others. They gave us a proverbial "face." That we jump at every opportunity to make an easy social connection isn't so surprising, considering that God has hardwired us for relationships. Perhaps it's because the digital social media we have developed taps perfectly into our DNA and fuels our desire for connection and attachment.

The downside to all this digital connection is it's not as perfect as we would like it to be. Many experts have drawn attention to the fact that in the digital world we only experience "pseudo connections" as a society, not the face-to-face relationships that God intended. If our social connections are not in-the-flesh, face-to-face social connections, we will feel increasingly lonely. Our wonderful brain responds better to reality and face-to-face connectivity more than to any other form of social connection.

Living in the Shallows

There are researchers who also believe that life in the digital world is causing us to lose our "depth"—our depth of thinking, contemplation, feeling, and emotions, as well as depth in our relationships and work. There is an emerging recognition that this shallow depth in our cognitive processors is causing us a new range of problems. Our digital gadgets are so smart that we don't have to be so smart ourselves anymore. In short, it can make us dumb! We don't have to remember how to spell words, do math, or research a project. We can get any answer we need with the click of a mouse.

As a professor that teaches PhD students, I (Dr. Hart) have noticed several changes in the lecture room over the past five years. For instance, graduate students don't want to be challenged to reason anything or figure out a problem anymore. "Just give me the answer" is the dominant attitude. Rote learning has taken over what used to be reasoned learning. I recently presented a class with a psychological test that required them to integrate several concepts I had been teaching, in order to arrive at a diagnosis of a hypothetical case. An outspoken student was quite blunt, telling me that he didn't have time to sit down and reason things out. All he wanted was for me to tell him where he can find the answer in the textbook.

Our ability to reflect and reason seems to be declining. It appears that while modern technology is fantastic in being able to give us instant answers, this easy access to a lot of information is also reshaping our creativity, inventiveness, and ingenuity. The result? According to Dr. Nicholas Carr, an expert in this area, it is making us shallow thinkers. And he is also convinced that shallow thinking will lead to shallow living.

What is "depth" as opposed to "shallow" in this context? By "depth" we mean a quality of awareness or understanding that comes when we truly engage some serious aspect of our life experience. Everything that happens to us all day long, every sight and sound, every personal encounter, every thought that crosses our minds, is a candidate for "depth." These all get lost in a shallow life. As William Powers says in his book *Hamlet's Blackberry*, "This is not a small matter. It's a struggle that's taking place at the center of our lives. It's a struggle *for* the center of our lives, for control of how we think and feel. When you're scrambling all the time, that's what your inner life becomes: scrambled. Why are we doing this to ourselves? Do we really want a world in which everyone is staring at screens all the time, keeping one another busy? Is there a better way?"[6] Yes, we happen to believe there is a better way, and hopefully we will be able to point you the reader in that direction.

Wake-Up Call to Parents

How is your family's relationship with technology doing? Consuming media, it seems, has far outstripped reading storybooks or playing dress-up as the average American child's favorite pastime. It has been said that media today is the "other" parent. With kids spending an average of eight hours a day in the digital world and only two and a quarter hours a day with their parents, there's bound to be some challenge to the parenting task.[7] The other night my (Dr. Frejd's) son Daniel, who I am always trying to pull back into real life, wanted to show me some card tricks that he had learned (online, of course). I was writing away on my laptop and honestly did not have the time or the inclination to be interrupted. As he started to walk away, obviously disappointed, I thought to myself, *OK, this is exactly what you are writing about in your book. Parents need to manage their digital life so they can be better parents in helping their children manage their lives.* So I called Daniel to come back, closed the lid to my laptop, and spent the next hour watching my son demonstrate 56 card tricks (OK, maybe it was only 10!).

This incident was a real wake-up call to me. It was one of many as I have been writing this book. We doubt if there is any parent who does not need a wake-up call today. The impact of the digital world on our families is already enormous and out of control. For some, a wake-up call may already be too late. Nevertheless, we are issuing this call to all parents: set aside any preconceived ideas you might have about the influence of an out-of-control digital world, and be prepared to take control and manage your family's engagement of technology.

The digital invasion is also shaping our children's physical health. We are increasingly becoming more sedentary as a society. Do you know that your child has a one-in-three chance of developing Type 2 diabetes? Type 2 diabetes now strikes about 3,700 children per year. Twenty-four million people have diabetes and fifty-seven million people are pre-diabetic.[8] Eighteen percent of America's children are obese. Obesity rates for children have more than doubled in the last thirty years, the biggest increase coinciding with the advent of the Internet. These serious health issues ought to create concern for parents as they help navigate their children through this digital age.

Take Ellen, for example. When her daughters were younger, her diaper bag was filled with coloring books, crayons, storybooks, and little games, in case one of them became restless and needed to be occupied. Now that Ellen's kids are four and seven, the diaper bag is gone, but the need for entertainment, especially in restaurants, is not, which is why two-thirds of the apps on Ellen's iPhone are for her children. Our smartphones have become a combination of pacifier, security blanket, and babysitter.

Is this a good thing or a bad thing? Should Ellen allow her children to play apps on her cell phone when they need attention? And then for how long? These, and many more, are the questions now confronting parents.

In parenting my (Dr. Frejd's) teenage son, I have found it extremely challenging to monitor the time he spends in the digital world. It takes a lot of effort and time to be aware of what video games he is playing, how long he has been playing, what music he is listening to, what videos he is watching on YouTube, or who he is texting. It seems at times to be a full-time job! But I am realizing how important it is to win his trust as I try to help manage this digital world. It is my influence as his parent that trumps everything else.

Parents need to model good digital management themselves. Don't expect your family to toe the line when you abuse the technology yourself. In so doing you ensure that your family achieves the best possible outcome. We will offer many ideas on how you can do this later.

Wake-Up Call to Teachers and Educators

Just as parents need to wake up to what is going on in their digital world, teachers and educators also need to wake up to the battle going on in education across our country. Educationally based technology is impacting our students just as much as entertainment technologies, affecting the way they learn, think, and interact. Unfortunately, it seems that at the present time, experts are quite divided on what is educationally good, and what is bad or even destructive, to our children's learning. This means that educators need to pay careful attention to the research going on, and tread cautiously in what they embrace *and* in what they reject. We have a lot at stake when it comes to educating our children.

According to Dr. Cynthia Belar, the American Association Director for Education, "advances in technology have altered every facet of education, from the way we teach, to the pedagogy we use, to the way we manage classrooms."[9] Technology can help us engage students, gather their opinions, measure how much they are learning and even detect plagiarism. Higher education students and home-schooled students now take courses online, and virtual training, where the computer simulates a real life situation such as learning to fly an airplane, can speed the training and make it safer. (I sure wish I [Dr. Hart] had virtual training when I learned to fly.)

But in Dr. Belar's opinion, the field of education also needs "to consider . . . implementation, standards, evidence base, ethics and related legal issues" facing education in this new digital world.[10]

So, what issues do teachers and educators need to be aware of? Presenting at a recent conference for Christian teachers, I (Dr. Hart) was totally taken aback by the pressure that was being placed on teachers to become more "technologically centered" in their teaching. I was pleasantly surprised to see how smart the teachers were in exercising caution and not just jumping to accept every new technology or newfound strategy that was being proposed and marketed to make money. These teachers were fully aware of both the risks and benefits that technology seemed to offer the educational field. They seemed to have a grass roots, intuitive understanding that we should not charge full speed ahead and revise our teaching methods just to accommodate some sales pitch on newfangled digital technology. They were quite clear that we needed to know where the boundaries should be, and what is good and bad about this totally new approach to teaching.

Now don't misunderstand where we are coming from. The teaching benefits that digital technology has to offer are obvious. As a professor, I (Dr. Hart) use these tools all the time. What is more important at this early stage in transforming our educational methods is the question, How does the digital world impact the literacy and other basic skills of our kids? We don't really know, and research is only at the beginning stage of investigating how significant the changes to education are impacting us.

In an effort to better understand the ways in which young people's learning and expression are being shaped by mobile and digital technologies, the Pearson Foundation recently released a research white paper entitled "The Digital World of Young Children: Emergent Literacy." It explores the effects of digital media on young children's learning and was presented at the 2010 Consortium for School Networking International Symposium, in Washington, DC.[11] The authors were early childhood education experts and included Arizona State University's Jay Blanchard and Terry Moore. The paper they presented examines the latest research on the ways in which young children make use of mobile media—including cell phones, television, video games, smart devices, and computers, and how they impact new ways of learning. Their research findings are quite optimistic and the highlights can be summarized as follows:

• Developmental milestones are changing as a new generation of young children approach learning and literacy in ways not thought possible in the past.

• Digital media is already transforming the language and cultural practices that enable early literacy development, making possible a new kind of personal and global interconnectedness.

What the report does not emphasize is the need for new research that reassesses the threats posed by technology to the social, emotional, and physical development of children. In other words, while we might be gaining some ground in teaching basic science or technological skills, is this at the expense of losing qualitative thinking or reasoning skills?

Research also needs to examine the impact of technology in both formal and informal learning contexts, covering a range of technologies. One of the basic questions I (Dr. Hart) would like answered is whether reading books from an electronic device is equivalent in learning value to reading a real book. Personally, I don't get much of a thrill from an electronic reading device, but that may be entirely due to the fact that I was raised on paper books where pages could be folded, you could write comments in the margin, jump backward and forward easily, and it smelled like a book!

More seriously, while we know that there are serious problems with "multiple tasking" and other distracting behaviors, we still don't know enough about the social and cultural issues that affect learning using technology.

Yes, the digital world is here to stay. Our classrooms are being rewired big time, and these changes will reshape how our children learn. Like it or not, we are headed for some major revisions. We believe that, in this period of transition, we need to pay careful attention to the consequences of this modified learning.

Another report worthy of attention is the "2011 Cisco Connected World Technology Report." This study asked students and young professionals in fourteen countries about their media consumption habits and impact on the workplace. These are the findings:

• Cisco surveyed 1,441 18- to 24-year-old college students and about 1,400 young professionals in their 20s. More than half of the college students and young professionals said that "they could not live without the Internet, it is an integral part of their daily life."

- The younger generation also said they could not live without their mobile devices including smartphones, laptops, and tablets; 66 percent of students and 55 percent of young professionals said mobile devices are the "most important technology in their lives."

- Among students, 40 percent considered the Internet to be more important than social activities, including dating and spending time with friends. "If forced to choose, two out of three college students would choose Internet connection instead of a car."[12]

The survey also asked students about the distractions the Internet created: 43 percent of students reported that the social media interrupts their studying three or more times per hour; 84 percent said social media, mobile phones, or IMs interrupted their studies at least once in an hour. In our opinion, over the long haul, and with intensity increasing every day, such digital disruptions are bound to have a detrimental learning effect, especially for less disciplined children—that is, if educators and parents don't enforce limited and disciplined use of the social media during homework or study time.

Another resource worth mentioning, as we examine issues that educators need to be aware of, comes from Pulitzer Prize–winning author Matt Richtel. He spent four months at high schools in California's Silicon Valley, observing how technology was shaping young people's lives. His report is not so positive, but does help us discover what some of the important issues are that we are facing. He sees a new set of social types now emerging among the young. It's not the showoff or the jock anymore, but the texter, gamer, Facebook addict, and YouTube potato. He interviewed a number of students, and their responses reflect widespread activities on the part of students:[13]

- One student: "I text while I am doing everything. I had 27,000 text messages last month." Her phone has played a "bad role" in her homework and grades. She tries to study, but then she gets a text message and has to reply right away. Then she checks Facebook and returns to her homework later, but she has already forgotten what she was reading earlier, so she has to start all over again.

- Another student: "Technology has been bad for me as a student, but good for me as a learner." He likes learning on Google or

YouTube at his own speed, about what he wants to know, not what the teacher has assigned him. He says that, after three or four hours researching online, "I feel like I've accomplished more for myself than, like, sitting down and writing an essay." Such a feeling will be the only accomplishment if the value of essay writing is completely undermined by technology.

* Another student observed that the "old way" of teaching wasn't working anymore. Cell phones, Facebook, and video games have conditioned him and his friends to experience "instant gratification," something traditional learning doesn't always provide.

* One of the schools studied tried to restrict cell phones on campus. The principal's conclusion? It didn't work. Taking the cell phones away from the teenagers was like taking away one of their limbs. Their cell phones are a part of their body. This is not very promising. Currently the school is trying to find a balance between utilizing technologies wherever appropriate, and also teaching teachers and students moderation in their use of technology. And, we might add, there is a long way for us to go before we achieve the right balance between new technology-based learning and traditional learning!

In our research, we found that many schools around the country were introducing their students to iPods or iPod touches early in their studies, and having them carry it with them throughout the day, not just utilizing them in every class they attend. This has created a greater debate about whether this is a positive move or a negative one. As a teacher and educator, you will have to decide how technology can serve you and your students instead of you serving it. Whichever side of the battle you end up on, our advice is that it is extremely important that you know the facts and stay as up-to-date as you possibly can on how technology impacts young minds, and what you can do about it. We are not advocating getting rid of technology. Rather, we are pleading for greater wisdom in how to use it. One of the most important facts to keep in mind is that the young mind needs to rest. Even an adequate sleep cycle is essential to learning. And it is very clear that our current overuse of the digital world does not increase the sleep cycle, nor does it allow the brain to slow down and disengage when it needs to. The young brain cannot function efficiently with information overload.

Questions for Teachers to Reflect On

1. What does good digital citizenship practice look like in my classroom and community?
2. How can I help my students develop a sense of ethics and responsibility when social networking?
3. Should my students be allowed to have access to their cell phones in my classroom?
4. Do these communication methods fit in an educational setting? What positive outcomes do they enable?
5. Is it appropriate for teachers to allow Facebook in the classroom so that students can communicate with each other online?

A Rainbow in the Dark Skies of Learning

In researching the relationship between technology and education, we did find a rainbow in the dark skies of learning. Just a few days ago the *New York Times* reported that the chief technology officer of eBay now sends his children to a nine-classroom school where technology is totally omitted.[14] Yes, you read correctly, "technology is totally omitted." But that is not all. So do the employees of Silicon Valley giants like Google, Apple, Yahoo, and Hewlett-Packard. The schools they go to use teaching tools that are anything but high-tech. They use old-fashioned pens and paper and a blackboard with different-colored chalk. Remember these? There's not a computer to be found anywhere. They are not allowed in the classroom, and the school even frowns on their use at home. This is quite a contrast to the thousands of schools nationwide that have rushed to supply their classrooms with computers and other digital gadgets. Many technology-focused educators believe that it is foolish to do otherwise.

There is now a growing awareness on the part of educators and parents, especially those who are close to technology companies such as in the Silicon Valley, that *computers and schools don't mix*. While they offer some new ways of learning, they are too distracting in other areas. To be honest, we strongly suspect that they could be right. The parents of the children in high-tech schools were reporting that about half of the children on computers in classrooms spend more of their time on Facebook, not on learning.

The new brand of schools that offers "non-computer-based education" is called "Waldorf Schools." No doubt there will be many others who will follow. There are already about 160 Waldorf schools nationwide. Their main educational philosophy focuses on physical activity, interpersonal engagement, and learning through creative, hands-on tasks. Those who endorse this approach say computers inhibit creative thinking, movement, human interaction, and attention spans. In essence, the Waldorf method of teaching is nothing other than what teachers used to do before the digital invasion.

What we cannot ignore in the debate over technology's influence in education is the fact that many technology experts themselves who are deeply rooted in scientific technology and its practice support this anti-tech learning perspective. The NY Times article reports one expert's opinion as follows:

> "I fundamentally reject the notion you need technology aids in grammar school," said Alan Eagle, 50, whose daughter, Andie, is one of the 196 children at the Waldorf elementary school. . . . "The idea that an app on an iPad can better teach my kids to read or do arithmetic, is ridiculous."[15]

These are strong words. If this approach continues to grow, we could see a dramatic change for the better. However, there will most certainly be those who question the old-fashioned form of education, and there will undoubtedly be an ongoing debate about the future role of computers in the classroom. Hopefully we will reach some sort of balance before it is too late. It is very possible that, in the future, schools like the Waldorfs may offer, say, one class period a day that is dedicated to developing computer skills, while in the rest of the day use nondigital education tools. Not a bad compromise!

Wake-Up Call to Pastors and Chaplains

The advent of the digital world and its many distractions is bound to have an impact on pastors and churches. Internet social networking, PlayStations, smartphones, iPods, iPads, and a host of other digital gadgets are now a fact of life. They are here to stay. But they have crept up so suddenly that the church and its leaders have not been equipped to sift through the digital tsunami and sort out the good from the bad. Many eagerly jumped on the tech wagon believing that it would be a new and better way to spread the gospel. After all, the church has historically been a devourer of new technology, embracing printing centuries ago, and live radio. (I [Dr. Hart], grew up in South Africa listening to "The Old-Fashioned Revival Hour" program of Charles Fuller, never ever imagining that one day I would be a professor at the seminary named after him.) Then television came along and we embraced that as a way to reach out to the world. And by-and-large the church and missionary organizations have used these technologies appropriately and effectively.

But does the digital invasion, which we have also eagerly embraced, have the same promise? Should we be more cautious, or does it have greater risks embedded in it compared to previous technologies?

According to a colleague at Fuller Theological Seminary, Dr. Carolyn Gordon, chair of the Department of Preaching and Communication,

> One of the problems associated with adopting use of new technologies is that many churches and other religious organizations and institutions have jumped headlong into the quickly moving stream, investing vast amounts of money in new technologies that they often knew little about.[16]

We agree that pastors need to raise their awareness and, as Dr. Gordon advocates, "*view digitally mediated ministry with a critical eye.*" However, we would add that pastors and churches must also pay attention to the growing new psychopathologies and health issues that come in the wake of the excessive use of digital technology. We are experiencing an exploding problem of added addictions; children are being robbed of sleep so that their learning is compromised; marriages are being destroyed by Internet pornography and cybersex; and much more.

The challenges facing pastors as they try to minister to people caught up in the digital world are enormous. Their congregations need guidance in how they should engage the digital technology that surrounds them and their children. Many pastors have expressed to us the tremendous expectations being placed on them to answer emails and texts instantly from their congregation. It is imperative that pastors address these issues with their congregation. At present, very little help is being offered within the church. The reason is obvious: parents and pastors are uncertain about what is good and what is bad in modern technology. Where should they set the boundaries for Internet and cell phone use at home and in church? Already, some experts are claiming that our mobile phones are becoming more like a "Frankenstein's monster," due mainly to our increasing addiction and inability to keep it under control. It doesn't help when the church overlooks this lack of control. Imagine how challenging it is going to become to control our digital gadgets in the years to come.

Our message is very simple: Church leaders and pastors need to step to the front of the line and take the lead in guiding our ethical and moral use of the Internet. Its impact can only be a positive one if we stay fully informed and manage our engagement of the digital world responsibly.

Digital Addiction in the Military

We had the privilege of speaking with Major Mark Awdykowyz a chaplain in the military, and he shared with us how the digital world is invading our armed forces:

> I believe that addressing this problem should become the cornerstone for reducing suicide in the military. Most of our military population under 25 years of age doesn't have the coping skills to successfully process trauma, rejection, failure, loss, and major life changes. The relational piece that involves an emotional and spiritual connection with other healthy people is missing. In addition, the large majority of our military chapels are failing at reaching our military population. Commanding Generals of Army installations are putting pressure on their Garrison Chaplain to reach soldiers and become part of the solution to reducing our high suicide rates.
>
> Personnel in the Active Army have endured multiple deployments into combat zones over the last ten years. Many have averaged 3 to 4 twelve-month combat tours in this time frame. The stress of improvised explosive devices (IED) on a daily basis, seeing friends and battle buddies killed or dismembered, along with the multiple separations from family, has many people scrambling for relief. Internet pornography is virtually everywhere—male and female alike—home and in the barracks. Gaming, sexting, texting, and hook-up sites are commonplace for many soldiers under 25 years of age. Our young marriages are falling apart: domestic violence is on the rise (just published last month) and the Army has a higher sexual assault rate than the other three services combined. The Obama administration has produced mandatory Army briefings that state, "Homosexually is not immoral, it's an alternate

lifestyle." All this is to say that digital technology has invaded our social norms, culture, and people's personality.

The USA has the most advanced military in the world and our soldiers, marines, airmen, and sailors are doing a great job at defeating our nation's enemies. Unfortunately, most of them are failing miserably at making life work and finding meaningful, satisfying relationships outside the battlefield. The only community they know is the one they experience downrange in a war zone. When they return home, they reach for the Xbox and the Internet, and fail at meaningful connections with their spouse, children, extended family, and the community. The end result is a significant rise in suicide, sexual assault, and domestic violence.

What Pastors and Chaplains Can Do about It

1. Plan on regularly addressing the theological and philosophical aspects of our digital world. Ignorance is Satan's greatest weapon. Christians today deserve a clear, trustworthy understanding of the limitations and consequences of our digital invasion.

2. Plan regular sermons or congregational meetings at which digital myths can be addressed and updated research offered on the effects of digital overuse. Place a special emphasis on how addictions can be so easily formed in our digital world. If necessary, regularly bring in an expert to keep you and your church well informed.

3. Help your church learn to be better stewards of their own digital technology. They need to know how to set boundaries for Internet or gaming usage and foster more face-to-face family interactions.

4. While both native and immigrant digital populations are becoming deeply involved in social networking, like Twittering and Facebooking, they need to be shown how to be good stewards of their time. Social media is a time guzzler and it can easily draw your people to social institutions outside of the church. If certain church members are in need of friends or are lonely (and our churches are full of lonely people), the church community needs to step forward and provide these friendships. Because we are failing to do this, social networking systems draw many away. Perhaps each church should develop its own social networking system so as to help those who are lonely.

5. Lastly, provide counseling and support groups to those who need help in overcoming their digital addiction problems. Train lay counselors to help others in developing appropriate Internet habits and etiquette. In South Korea, children are taught "netiquette" (appropriate ways of behaving on the Internet) in the very first year of schooling. Surely our children deserve the same.

Discussion Questions

1. Have you experienced a "wake-up call" moment, like Mark had in the opening? What was the outcome?

2. How is technology changing your life, for good and for bad?

3. What do you think about the "Waldorf" schooling system that bans all computers from the classroom? What are its positives, and what are its negatives?

4. What did you think of this statement: "There is no doubt that our wonderful brain is better suited to deal with reality and face-to-face connectivity than to some Internet connection."

5. How is the use of your technology reshaping your creativity?

6. As a parent, what are some of the concerns you have in parenting a child in this digital age?

3

The Rewiring of
Our Brains

Imagine the brain, that shiny mound of being, that mouse-gray parliament of cells, that dream factory, that petit tyrant inside a ball of bone, that huddle of neurons calling all the plays, that little everywhere, that fickle pleasure-drome, that wrinkled wardrobe of selves stuffed into the skull like too many clothes into a gym bag.

Diane Ackerman, *An Alchemy of Mind*

When the rest of the world thinks we are idle, the brain, if properly trained, is following its own path.

Bertrand Russell, *In Praise of Idleness*[1]

You've heard the expression "Change your brain, change your life." It became popular when a dear friend, Dr. Daniel Amen, published his book on this topic. "Changing your brain" has always had a positive connotation, as if every change you can make to your brain is for the better.[2] Yes, our brain is changing, but it might not be changing for the better, at least not if we don't take control of how we are changing it. For this reason, we believe that a basic understanding of how we are changing our brain is essential to understanding the risks that our digital world poses for future generations. So whether you are an educator, pastor, or parent, we want to lay out some basic brain principles that are being modified as we engage the digital world. We will try to keep it simple and understandable, but ignoring this information can put you and your children at risk for some digitally caused brain changes that may not be for the better.

The brain is an astonishing organ. It is also central to everything the digital world has to offer. Our Internet world is expanding so rapidly that research can barely keep up with its impact. In a sense, what we want to emphasize is how important it is for us to protect the brain, the most vulnerable part of the body, as we embrace all the good the cyber world has to offer.

Are Our Brains Changeable?

We begin with this question because the biggest concern to scientists studying the effect of the digital invasion is that it will inevitably change the way our brain works. So how much can it change? Does it have any form of inbuilt protection? Are there limits to how much it can change? Will the change always be for our good, or can it turn us into monsters?

As with all challenges, there are two sides to the debate. There are the "digital optimists" who believe that the change will always be for the good. They want us to engage every aspect of change that our wonderful new cyber world has to offer. They accept everything about technology uncritically, and see any opposition to this acceptance as being equal to the doomsday predictions of the inventions of previous eras. They cite the advent of bicycles, radios, movies, and television as examples of new technologies that were tainted with doom. They believe that while these inventions may have initially caused some dramatic changes in lifestyle, their usage ultimately became commonplace and life assumed a new normal. There was no doomsday consequence.

So, does this mean we are overreacting when we predict dire consequences for our cyber-invasion? Before we can come to any definite for or against conclusion, we need to explore the vulnerability of the brain a little further.

There was a time when we believed that the brain was unchangeable. That once it matures, it could not change. For example, you might be able to learn to play the piano or master a new language, but the brain remained essentially the same throughout life. We even believed that when brain cells died, they could not be replaced. Now we know differently. There is a part of the brain called the *hippocampus* that manufactures more than a million new brain cells every day. Neurologists have now embraced the concept that the brain is plastic and can even repair itself. This phenomenon is called *neuroplasticity* and refers to the brain's susceptibility to change under certain conditions, such as changes in behavior, in our environment, or after the loss of certain parts of the brain. In fact, the brain is constantly changing throughout your life. Are these changes our digital world is making in our brain all for good and how far can we take this change? Is there a point at which the change becomes destructive and likely to affect the brains of our offspring? These are the questions facing scientists today. Moreover, as we will see, the answers are not very positive. We have reason to pause here and take stock of where we are going so that we will be able to set up healthier ways for engaging our digital world.

To have a complete understanding of how our brain can change under the influence of the cyber world, we need to start at birth. A baby's brain contains 100 billion neurons (brain cells). This is roughly equivalent to the number of stars in the Milky Way. It produces these neurons before birth and then continues after birth to grow connections between them. During the first years of life, the brain continues to undergo a series of extraordinary changes. For instance, with very little help, and simply by mimicking others, a child miraculously learns to speak a language. By the time the child reaches the teenage years, there are more neurons in the brain than needed, so the brain starts a "pruning process" to eliminate connections that are seldom or never used.

Yes, our brain is extraordinary! There is nothing else in the universe that matches its complexity. Evidence suggests that the brain is changing more rapidly now than ever before in history. Some have referred to this change as an "artificial, accelerated evolution," but do not see every change that the digital world has to offer our wonderful, God-given brain as being for the better. We agree with those who believe that the change now taking place is far too rapid and vast in its extent to be beneficial. Dr. Gary Small, director of the Memory and Aging Center at UCLA, puts it this way:

> While the brains of today's Digital Natives are wiring up for rapid-fire cyber searches, the neural circuits that control the more traditional

learning methods are neglected and gradually diminished. The pathways for human interaction and communication weaken as customary one-on-one people skills atrophy.[3]

No doubt, new technologies will continue to be added to our digital world for the rest of the world's existence. Some of these may help increase our intelligence, making us a little smarter than we are now. But, some will increase our propensity for addiction and undermine our basic humanness. Future generations of educators will be faced with monumental challenges. Just think about the impact that "abbreviated texting," will have on future generations' ability to spell. It is possible that at some time in the future there will be no need for children even to learn spelling, since all gadgets will be voice activated and do the spelling for us. How users spell words will not matter at all. Computers will correct all our errors, just as, or better, than they do now as we write.

But is this a healthy outcome? Many do not think so. It is more likely that the brain's basic structure and functioning could be modified to such an extent that it cannot revert to earlier functioning. In other words, once we have lost the art of spelling, we may never be able to retrieve it. As Nicholas Carr, a finalist for the Pulitzer Prize in General Non-fiction in 2011, puts it:

> We've always had external sources of information that supplemented our memory, but it seems to me that the danger here is that if we, in effect, train our brains to forget rather than to remember you may still be able to find the individual bits of information when you need them, but what you lose is the personal associations that happen when you actually go through the process of remembering something.[4]

This comment raises this question: Is it possible that neglect of some brain mechanisms, due to our overdependence on digital technology, could change our brain to such an extent that it will never function again as it used to? According to scientists like Dr. Small, this could happen.

Does the Brain Have Any Limitations?

Like it or not, despite our eagerness to embrace and train the brain to be better at tasks like multitasking and speed learning, our brains have very limited capacity for processing information.[5] The new tasks we learn may seem faster, but the rest of the brain may not be able to keep up.

The idea that the brain has limitless capacity for technological training and expansion is being questioned. As our technology expands, the limitations of what our brains can do will become more obvious. This limitation has implications for the way educators and industry are pushing us toward developing skills like multitasking. The idea that the human brain is capable of doing a zillion things at the same time has no validity, as we will see in chapter 4 when we discuss the myths of multitasking.

All of God's creation has limitations, and respecting these limitations is our responsibility. It is called "stewardship." At a recent conference of teachers, I (Dr. Hart) heard a number of educators touting the importance of training our kids to multitask. I cringed! They urged the group to embrace digital change, and no one seemed aware of the warnings that science is already reporting. Even though two simple tasks can be performed relatively simultaneously, when you perform multiple tasks, one of the tasks will suffer. The more tasks you perform, the more all will suffer.[6]

On the human intelligence side of things, many scientists say we may be close to the brain's evolutionary limit. We are certainly close to its created limits! Various lines of research suggest that most of the tweaks that could make us smarter will hit biological limits. For instance, the size of the brain is limited to the size of the skull, so it is not likely to grow bigger. It is also "energy-hungry" and slow. Just to keep up with technology our head size would have to increase dramatically. Maybe that is why aliens from other planets are always depicted as having enormous heads.

Some see the future not so much as humans growing grotesque heads, but as humans achieving a higher level of intelligence by coupling the brain with external processors and additional memory. Already technology has become micro-sized. We can put a lot of processing power on the head of a pin. The next step, in some minds, will be to link our brain to this additional processing power by expanding our brain's connection outside the confines of the skull. We may not live to see it; but scenarios like this are a powerful reminder that we need to control how technology affects our lives, starting with what we hold in our hands right now.

Brain Systems That Could Be Affected
by Our Hyper-Tech World

Today's youth, the most techno-savvy of any generation to date, have grown up surrounded by and dependent on computers and the Internet. They go to school equipped with the latest generation of smartphones and fully embrace the digital world with its constant flow of information.

But what systems in the brain are being affected by our digital technology? An understanding of these major systems can help us figure out what the possible long-term consequences could be from the overload. To help our readers understand the risks of excessive digital engagement, we will provide a brief overview of several of the brain's systems that we believe need particular protection. Every expert we have encountered says the same as Dr. Jordan Grafman, chief of Cognitive Neuroscience at the National Institute of Neurological Disorders:

> Technology in general can be good [for children's cognitive development] if it is used judiciously. But if it is used in a nonjudicious fashion, it will shape the brain in what I think will actually be a negative way.[7]

The more you know about these systems, the better equipped you will be to manage them in you and your children's lives. Because our space is limited, we will describe only six of them.

System One: The Brain's "Pleasure System"

Do you ever wonder what part of your brain gives you the feeling of pleasure? It is possibly the most important brain system of all because its misuse is the primary cause of the many Internet and gaming addictions that are generated by our digital world. Called the "Nucleus Accumbens," or popularly known as the "pleasure center," it is the part of the brain that controls every experience of pleasure. Whether it is a good meal, reading a first-rate book, or just sitting and holding the hand of someone you love, signals are sent to this part of the brain and it automatically delivers the feeling of pleasure or joy.

Just like many other things in life where excess is not best, overdosing the pleasure system can have very detrimental consequences. In particular, it is the overloading abuse of this pleasure center that lies behind many of the Internet addictions that now surround us. This topic is covered more fully in my (Dr. Hart's) book, *Thrilled to Death: How the Endless Pursuit of Pleasure Is Leaving Us Numb*.[8] Not only can overloading this system rob us of pleasures in the little things of life, but abusing it can also rob us of the "joy" that God promises us. The region of the brain that provides the sensation of pleasure is among the most fascinating. It is a system that rewards certain behaviors, which are good, so that you will repeat them. But if the pleasure system is overused, the experience of pleasure is diminished. You are then driven to seek a higher level of stimulation. As an example, let us imagine you are playing a video game. You initially spend half an hour playing the game, and it gives you a lot of pleasure. If you keep playing the game, however, the pleasure system becomes overloaded and starts to diminish the pleasure you experience. Now it demands even more game playing just to give a little pleasure. Therefore, you have to give increasing amounts of time to game playing just to keep the pleasure flowing. To put it simply, overloading the pleasure system gradually raises the bar so that you have to increase the level of stimulation to maintain the pleasure. This phenomenon is called the *addictive process*. It is the basic cause of all addictions.

Dopamine is the basic neurotransmitter (chemical messenger) that carries the signal to your pleasure center from different parts of the brain. As you go for more and more pleasure, you push the dopamine level higher and higher. This is called *dopamine flooding*, and it creates a spiraling effect that results in compulsive drug or behavior abuse.

Many of our Internet behaviors, such as gambling or gaming on the Internet, or even Facebooking, can do as much damage to the pleasure center as any powerful drug. The pleasure center can become so flooded that only the "big" stimulants can get a message to the pleasure center. Little, ordinary pleasures are ignored because they do not have the power to overcome the flooding. This loss of ability to experience ordinary pleasure is called *anhedonia*, and it can create serious emotional disorders. In fact, anhedonia is one of the main symptoms of major depression.

What this all means is that the thrills of our digital world, if abused, can be as addicting as any drug and rob you of the simple joys of life.

How can we prevent our digital world from causing these addictions? By giving our pleasure system regular breaks in order to restore its balance. If the brain does not get some downtime, it cannot function as it should. Have you ever wondered why watching a beautiful sunset no longer gives you pleasure, or why sitting in a shady garden with singing birds surrounding you gives you no joy? Or why seeing a rainbow after a storm once filled you with wonder but now is "dull and boring"? It's because we have too many other pleasures flooding our pleasure center. Excessive digital use overloads the pre-frontal cortex, the part of the brain that operates self-regulation. Because of this inability to self-regulate, we spend more time in our digital life. The more time spent in the digital world, the less ability we have to self-regulate.

One of the world leaders in dealing with digital technology's addictions is the government of South Korea. They have been at the forefront in developing technology, and now realize that they have a national problem. Many hundreds of young people go to the popular large "gaming auditoriums" scattered around their cities, playing games for hours on end, becoming addicted to the pleasure they derive from their gaming. Many play games all through the night, and then stagger to school or work the next day. A few incidents have been reported where the gamers became so engrossed in their gaming activity that they would not break for food or even go to the bathroom, and were found dead, slumped over their gaming computers. As a result, the South Korean government has been the first to confront the problem of gaming addiction and has taken steps to clamp down on Internet misuse. They are setting an example for the rest of the world to follow.

System Two: The Brain's "Tranquility System"

A close neighbor of the brain's pleasure center is the system that offers us tranquility. When this system malfunctions we experience severe anxiety.

How does it work? The chemical messengers here are the natural tranquilizers that the brain manufactures. They target receptors scattered throughout the brain to give us the sense of peace and tranquility. When there is an abundance of these natural tranquilizers, all the receptors are being comforted. When these tranquilizers are depleted, our anxiety goes up and can reach a level that creates panic anxiety.

It is well known that a "tranquilizer," in pharmacological terms, is a drug that calms the brain and relieves anxiety. The first synthesized tranquilizer, called Librium, was invented in the 1950s, and it has revolutionized the treatment of anxiety disorders. At the time it was invented, scientists had no idea how tranquilizers worked. Only later did they discover that the brain actually manufactures its own tranquilizers, equivalent to those we use as medications. The reason why artificial tranquilizers work is because they target the same receptors as the brain's natural tranquilizers.

But what does this have to do with our digital invasion? Simply put, the constant stimulation of the brain by our overused techno-gadgets causes a stress hormone called *cortisol* to increase. Excessive, unneeded cortisol can block important tranquility receptors, causing the brain to shut down its production of natural tranquilizers. Therefore, understanding how the digital world can cause excessive cortisol arousal and can affect our sense of peacefulness is very important.

Cortisol is produced by the adrenal glands in response to any excitement or demand. This means that many digital applications, like gaming, texting, tweeting, and even Facebooking, can cause a stress response that results in cortisol elevation. In fact, wherever you see stress, you will see cortisol in abundance. All computer games are designed to give you an adrenal kick, and whenever adrenaline goes up, cortisol does also. A part of cortisol's function is to block the tranquility receptors so as to make you more anxious and prepare you to deal with an emergency. Only, it isn't a real emergency but instead a game-induced emergency. This loss of tranquility can lead to more serious anxiety disorders. This is all described in more detail in my (Dr. Hart's) book, *The Anxiety Cure*.[9]

There is no doubt that the excessive and prolonged use of our digital technology can elevate our cortisol level when overused. Cortisol's function is basically to protect and assist us in dealing with anything that is stressful, but the "emergency" may be nothing more than our smartphone's ringing. The persistent elevation of cortisol, such as we see in digital addictions or multitasking, can also increase your risk of serious health disorders, including obesity, Type 2 diabetes, high blood pressure, and heart disease.

What is the antidote for this cortisol assault and loss of tranquility? There are four recommended solutions for preventing your digital world from robbing you of your tranquility and creating an anxiety disorder:

> **First,** limit the time you spend on the Internet or your smartphone. Restrict your use of stimulating gadgets, websites, or gaming.
>
> **Second,** maintain a regular program of physical exercise. Generally, we are too sedentary, and the digital world has made us even

less mobile. Physical exercise helps to burn off adrenaline and reduce cortisol levels.

Third, practice deep muscle relaxation exercises. It is widely acknowledged that these relaxation exercises can help reduce the effects of our stress hormones—including cortisol. (Information on how to get Dr. Hart's Relaxation Training audio CD is provided in appendix F.)

Fourth, enhance your brain's natural tranquilizers. This is achieved mainly by improving your sleep habits. There is abundant evidence that excessive Internet use can disturb our sleep habits. Teenagers often engage in texting in the late-night hours and quickly become insomniacs. Even a slight improvement in sleep quality and quantity can work wonders.

System Three: The Brain's "Memory System"

Dr. Torkel Klingberg, professor of cognitive neuroscience, and many other experts are telling us that the human brain has a very "limited memory system." New findings in psychology and brain research indicate that much of how we process the information the digital world throws at us, with its distractions, demands for multitasking, and simultaneous processing, has one serious side effect: it reduces our ability to retain information.[10]

Many digital tasks now require you to do more than one thing at a time or to jump from one task to another. The first task in the chain demands a certain amount of "working memory." The second task in the chain now demands double the amount of memory. The question that arises is, just how much memory can the brain process at the same time when there are multiple demands? What is clear is that the human brain is a lot more limited in "working memory" than most of us realize, and this can lead to certain serious consequences if we place too many demands on it. For example, a surgeon who tries to multitask while performing complicated tasks could make a major error and jeopardize someone's life. We face the same challenge when we drive fast on the freeway, a relatively uncomplicated task. Jumping from lane to lane in an unfamiliar city while trying to follow directions on a GPS complicates the task exponentially. If we make too many changes, our brain cannot remember all the details. The bottom line is this: We function best and most efficiently when we do **one task at a time.**

System Four: The Brain's "Learning System"

Closely tied to the memory system is the learning system. It is important to remember that all learning is brain-based. The process of education is literally all about changing the brain, not other functions of the body. This does not mean that every parent or teacher needs to become a neuroscientist, memorize 100 neurotransmitters, or learn about the fifty areas of the brain responsible for learning so that they can become more effective as parents or teachers. But every parent and teacher needs to be aware of a few essential bits of information.

The first is called "neural system fatigue" or "brain fatigue." What this means is that, like all parts of our body, the system responsible for learning can also become fatigued. If we are too tired to focus attention on the material or skill being learned, no lasting learning can occur. But how does the digital world affect this? What our digital world offers us is an abundance of distraction, not in the healthy sense like taking up a hobby, but more in a disruptive sense. For example, the average child doing homework or reading an assigned book will probably have a cell phone close by. If a friend calls or texts, the child will become distracted and the learning process will be disrupted. Several disruptions like this can accentuate neural system fatigue. Neurology is very clear here: neural systems involved in learning are "fatigued" quite quickly, actually within minutes. They get tired and stop working. No real learning can take place when one is constantly being distracted. In short, whatever form they take, distractions place an additional load on the neural system that undermines learning.

Scientists are now pointing to another discovery that can disrupt the learning process. When people (and this includes our children) keep their brains busy with digital input, they forfeit *downtime*. Downtime is what the brain needs between learning tasks so that it can process and consolidate the information it is learning. This is not a fatigue problem but a lack-of-time-to-process problem.

Lack of downtime also disrupts creativity.[11] One study, carried out at the University of Michigan, found that people learned significantly better if they took a walk after being exposed to some new learning, rather than just going on learning. If they took a walk in a noisy, crowded urban area, their learning was forgotten. But if it was a walk in the park or countryside, the learning was consolidated.[12] Digital engagement can interfere with downtime, so clearly, the more downtime we can give the brain between learning tasks, the better.

Finally, the last major disruption to the learning process we want parents and teachers to be aware of is lack of adequate sleep. Just as downtime or taking regular breaks and relaxing can enhance learning, so can healthy sleep. If the digital invasion has done anything significantly damaging to our world in general, it is that we have been robbed of much needed sleep. Sleep deprivation is a major learning killer. Why? Certain stages of sleep are essential to "cementing" in the brain what was learned the previous day.

The lack of sleep's effect on memory and the learning process is receiving a lot of research attention. Both animal and human studies suggest that both the quantity and quality of our sleep can have a profound impact on learning and memory. First, a sleep-deprived person is too fatigued the next day to focus attention on new material, and therefore cannot learn efficiently. Second, sleep itself plays a role in the consolidation of memory, which is essential for learning new information. Although there is no consensus about how sleep makes this process possible, many researchers think that specific characteristics of brainwaves during different stages of sleep are associated with the formation of particular types of memory.[13] Since sleep is so crucial to many health issues, in addition to its vital role in learning, we offer the following suggestions to help you and your children improve the quality of your sleep. The principles underlying each of the suggestions are explained in different sections of this book.

TEN WAYS TO IMPROVE SLEEP QUALITY

Copy this list and post it in a prominent place where all members of your family can see it.

1. Go to bed at the same time every night. The brain has to be programmed for consistent sleep onset.
2. Keep your bedroom as dark, quiet, and comfortable as possible. Use earplugs or an eye mask if necessary.
3. Drink no caffeine-based drink after 4:00 p.m. (preferably eliminate all caffeine). Caffeine blocks the brain's sedation receptors.
4. Learn a relaxation technique and use it when going to sleep.
5. About an hour before bedtime, turn down all lights and darken your environment. This helps start the production of melatonin, the brain's sleep hormone.

6. Do not engage in any activity after 8:00 p.m. Stay away from your computer or smartphone. That stimulates your adrenaline and prevents the onset of sleep.

7. Get up every morning at the same time (after having had enough sleep) and get into sunlight as soon as possible. This turns off your melatonin.

8. If you wake up at night, try not to get up. If you must, get back into bed as soon as possible and don't turn on any bright lights. Do your relaxation exercise.

9. Make sure you exercise or do enough physical work every day to make you tired. Physical fatigue helps sleep onset and burns off surplus adrenaline.

10. Work hard at stress management and de-stress yourself before going to bed. High stress is our greatest sleep killer.

You can get more detailed information on how to improve the quality of your sleep in Dr. Hart's book, *Sleep: It Does a Family Good*.[14]

System Five: The Brain's "Attachment System"

This system has not received a lot of attention, mainly because it is not as well understood as the others we have been discussing. It is also possible that most of our readers haven't given much thought to how their digital world is affecting how they attach to others, including family members.

God has hardwired our brains for attachment. Our first attachment should be to him. But *how* we "attach" ourselves to others in intimate relationships is the function of a particular brain system that is also under fire from the digital invasion. The reason we seek intimate relationships is that the attachment system in the brain prompts us to seek these intimate relationships with another person. It is what prompts us to seek a mate, get married, and have children. But not just in dating and falling in love, but also in forming friendships.

Let's face it: human relationships are complex and downright difficult at times. That's why we are inundated with self-help books, family therapists, and divorce.

We all, at some time or another, prefer to pick up the television remote or smartphone rather than have a face-to-face conversation with our spouse, child, or even co-workers. Sometimes connecting to the "virtual world" of the Internet is easier, less demanding, and more attractive than connecting to humans who have feelings that can be upsetting. Neuroscientist Gary Small describes it this way:

> Recent neuroscience points to pathways in the brain that are necessary to hone interpersonal skills, empathetic abilities, and effective personal instinct. In Digital Natives (our children) who have been raised on technology, these interpersonal neural pathways are often left unstimulated and underdeveloped. However, electronic overexposure leading to altered neural pathways and waning social skills can happen at any age. Digital Immigrants (older parents) also run the risk of becoming so immersed in the Internet and other new technologies that they experience a social and emotional distancing between themselves and their families and spouses.[15]

Human attachment is a biological need, without which we most likely could die. For thousands of years human beings have felt drawn to and lived in close, interactive communities. People spend a lot of time with other people. Our problem today is that while we may spend a lot more of our time with people, they are at the other end of a smartphone or on flat screens with no depth. This is not an improvement in our attachments. While technology is designed to improve human efficiency, it also has the effect of distancing humans from each other and changing our attachment styles.

Can we adapt to this growing sense of distance and isolation from real flesh and blood? What will be the impact on our youth who now have limited face-to-face interactions with parents and friends? The honest answer is that we don't really know. I (Dr. Hart) welcomed videophones and was an early member of Skype, just so I could talk to family members far away with a visible face. I think I have almost every app available for video contact through my iPhone, laptop, and tablets. They help me feel better connected. It is because I also have many direct physical contacts. Digital contacts can never compensate for real face-to-face human contact with those you love. The concern is this detachment's impact on how parents attach to children and in turn affect the attachment style they will develop. We are designed for real-life attachments where we are seen, valued, and heard. It is in our closest relationships that we experience this. If our brain system becomes more attached to digital gadgets and detached from people, our relational skills will atrophy. We are already seeing evidence of this.

With technology developing at such a fast pace, the only solution we have to this "detachment phenomenon" is to emphasize the importance of as much face-to-face contact and interaction as possible. Build in as many face-to-face encounters as you possibly can.

System Six: The Brain's "Spiritual System"

It would be remiss of us not to mention something about how the digital world is also affecting our Christian spirituality. We have interacted with many Christian groups, churches, and pastors and have a good idea of how our Christian lives are being impacted. Almost everywhere we have gone, whether to present at a conference or speak at a church, we come away with a strong feeling that "all is not good" in the Christian world. We see many church members fiddling with their smartphones during a worship service. There are those who get up and leave the service because their iPhone is vibrating from someone demanding instant attention. Not a pretty picture!

Pastors we know are also concerned about how intrusive cell phones are during church services. As a professor, I have banned all cell phones and online access with laptops from my lectures. Some pastors excuse smartphones, believing that church members may be using a Bible app to follow the sermon. More likely, members, especially the younger members, are playing games or texting others. One pastor shared with us that some of his members even criticized his sermons while he was preaching, by texting other church members or someone at home during the service. How disconcerting! Another pastor told us that he is seriously considering leaving the ministry because of these distractions.

What We Can Do about It

We have briefly described a few of the more important systems in our brains that can be impacted by the digital invasion. Understanding these systems can help you determine what sort of protective action you need to take. In the chapters to follow, we will expand on some of these solutions.

In closing this chapter, there is one extremely important point about all these systems we want to emphasize again: Just as the muscles in our physical body need to be rejuvenated by resting them from time to time, our brain also needs this rest time. In fact, our brain needs more downtime than the rest of our body. It is not that it is doing nothing during this downtime. Quite the contrary. It has many other functions to perform, such as solving problems, reasoning, fighting infections, repairing damage, and consolidating learning or memory, and can only perform these functions if given downtime.

The statement by Bertrand Russell quoted at the start of this chapter, taken from his book *In Praise of Idleness*, is right on target. Allow us to quote it again:

> When the rest of the world thinks we are idle, the brain, if properly trained, is following its own path.[16]

We are only really thinking when our brain is idle. It can't do much thinking when other demands take precedence. Unlike the idling engine of your automobile that is not achieving anything or going anywhere when the car is stopped, an idling brain is hard at work. A brain at rest is a thinking brain.

This is where the digital world loses many of its positive attributes. It does not take this need into account. If we allow the external world of digital technology to dominate our brain and not give it any "internal" time for itself, we will pay the price in reduced productivity and increased human misery. This is a strong statement, but we have ample reason for stating it.

To be healthy in mind and spirit in our digital go-go-go world, we need to find time for reflection and deliberation. We also need to give the brain adequate recovery time, meaning, of course, more sleep time. Otherwise, we can never truly think thoughts of our own. This is also true for our spiritual lives where contemplation, meditation, and other spiritual practices play a significant role.

This all boils down to one indisputable truth: God has created our brain with certain limitations. There is no space for extra memory or another processor. We must respect these limitations if we are going to thrive and live a healthy life. If we do not build rest and relaxation into our lives, we will become less effective thinkers and increase our stress and anxiety over the issues that stole our relaxation in the first place. When your brain gets the rest it needs, you learn better and become more creative.

As we will discuss in the next chapter, to be a genius in the future, you must be able to unplug on a regular basis and allow your brain to solve the great challenges facing it on its own. To be an ordinary, healthy person you must also be able to unplug regularly and rest "that mouse-gray parliament of cells, that dream factory, that petit tyrant inside a ball of bone, that huddle of neurons calling all the plays."[17]

Discussion Questions

1. Discuss what you learned about our brain's limitations.
2. What do you think about the statement, "When you perform more than one task, one of the tasks will suffer"? Explain.
3. Have you experienced an overloading of your pleasure system in using digital gadgets?
4. Which of the "Ten Ways to Improve Sleep Quality" on pages 68–69 do you need to apply to your life? How about to your family?
5. How has the digital world affected your relational attachments?
6. Would you like to allow your brain to have more idle time? What changes would you need to make to do this?

4

The Multitasking Myth

> There is time enough for everything in the course of the day, if you do but one thing at once, but there is not time enough in the year, if you will do two things at a time.
>
> Lord Chesterfield's letter to his son, 1747

These words, penned more than 260 years ago, are remarkably relevant to our modern digital age. Lord Chesterfield's stunning observation of the limits of the human brain needs to be heeded today, and has implications for what we now call *multitasking*. But his admonition is not just about how doing multiple things at the same time diminishes what you can achieve. In the letter Lord Chesterfield goes on to say: "This steady and undissipated attention to one object, is a sure mark of a superior genius; as hurry, bustle, and agitation, are the never-failing symptoms of a weak and frivolous mind."[1] Doing one thing at a time was, and still is, a mark of true intelligence.

Lord Chesterfield's comment is as applicable today as it was so long ago, especially since the advocates of our modern digital world are calling us all to become masters of multitasking. Wherever one turns, the rallying cry in education, business, and industry is *multitask*. But is multitasking all that it is cracked up to be? As we will see, our glorification of multitasking is not completely justified. We know of no researcher in this field who applauds multitasking. It is perceived by many to be a myth.

Yes, computers have helped us speed up things. I (Dr. Hart) can recall what a tremendous boost computerized statistical analysis was to my research. I could accomplish an enormous amount of work in a day, as compared to the tedious handheld calculators we previously had to use. Because we could do more things at once, the term *multitasking* emerged. We became experts in crowding, computing, packaging, and overlapping activities. Those that espoused multitasking started to talk about a "multitasking hotspot," as if we had enhanced the brain in some way.

Uncovering the Truth about Multitasking

What is the origin of the term *multitasking*? First, we must differentiate between computer multitasking and human multitasking. In computing, multitasking refers to the computer's ability to perform multiple tasks during the same period of time. Human multitasking is an individual appearing to perform more than one task at the same time. For example, a person can talk on the telephone while typing an email or knitting a pair of socks. Or you can drive your car while listening to music. Simple tasks that don't require anything to be remembered are easily done simultaneously.

In the early days of the computer, multitasking was considered an asset to human performance. More recently, the value of human multitasking, when involving more than just the simplest of tasks, is being seriously questioned. Some have gone so far as to describe human multitasking as a "mythical activity in which people believe they can perform two or more tasks simultaneously as effectively as one."[2] The very idea that our brains can perform many functions simultaneously without any penalty is being seen as a destructive force in human performance, learning, and even socializing. It has certainly become a critical issue that needs the attention of parents and educators, as we become a "multitasking generation."

While the introduction of multitasking made dull, repetitive work more exciting and took away boredom, it is not as productive as it claimed to be. In fact, several studies of multitasking have found multitasking to be significantly less productive than its alternative, called *sequential tasking*. In 2005, a study conducted by the Institute of Psychiatry at the University of London found that workers distracted by emails or phone calls suffered from a fall in their IQ level of 10 points, twice as much as found in marijuana smokers.[3] They called it "infomania" and predicted that job multitasking would become a major threat to workplace productivity. We are concerned that "infomania" might also invade our schools if we do not manage how children learn. As we have carefully reviewed the recent research surrounding multitasking, we have come to believe that the idea that multitasking facilitates better learning is one of the greatest myths surrounding the digital world.

No doubt, some readers at this point might be taking issue with our conclusion. Therefore, before we go much further, we want to clarify some of the terms that are being bandied about. There is clearly a semantic problem surrounding the term *multitasking*. It means different things to different people and this confuses our understanding of this phenomenon.

There is a difference between extreme multitasking and what might be called sequential tasking. While one might have multiple tasks to perform, such as mowing the lawn, weeding the garden, and washing the driveway, if you do them one at a time and finish each task before you move on to the next one, you are doing sequential tasking. If you have a large number of tasks to perform, but don't finish one before moving to the next, then return to the first task for a while, then jump to a third or fourth before going back to the first, you are multitasking. It is this "hopping about" from one task to another that is questionable.

This form of multitasking has been shown to be less productive than if you complete each task before going on to the next task, i.e., sequential tasking.[4] For example, I (Dr. Frejd) experienced this when I was a stay-at-home mom. A typical day would start out with me making lunches for the children, and then fixing breakfast, then driving the children to school, and then I would start a load of laundry, go on the Internet to pay some bills, answer the front door, and then start preparing for dinner. Here we have multiple tasks that must be performed. But even though some can be overlapped, like leaving the ironing to answer the front door and to transfer washing to the dryer, this is sequential tasking by and large, *not* the multitasking that is being embraced in our modern world. An example of true multitasking, as opposed to sequential tasking, is what happens when you drive your car on a busy downtown street, while you are trying to send a text message over your cell phone. We have now banned such behavior because we know it is dangerous. We all have multiple tasks to perform. But overlapping them can minimize our efficiency. What many advocates of multitasking omit is the brain's role in multitasking. The brain cannot fully focus when pushed to multitask. Therefore, it takes longer to complete tasks, and there is an increased likelihood you will make an error. This is because the brain is compelled to restart and refocus whenever it returns to the previous task. There are some researchers who have explored whether the human brain is capable of learning how to multitask more efficiently, especially if trained to do so at an early age. However, their findings show that while the brain can become more adept at processing information, it cannot truly multitask.[5]

Do Computers Really Multitask?

So much for human multitasking. But what about computers? Are they capable of real multitasking? Most people believe that computers are great multitaskers. Therefore, you might be surprised that we even ask such a question. Surely all computers multitask, otherwise how else could they possibly do so many things at the same time!

I (Dr. Hart) raised this question with my son-in-law, who happens to be a patent examiner at the United States Patent Office. He tells me that, strictly speaking, computers do not multitask. He referred me to Microsoft's *Computer Dictionary* that clearly describes how the average computer works.[6] The dictionary defines multitasking as "a mode of operation offered by an operating system in which a computer works on more than one task at a time." There are several types of multitasking. In "context switching," the computer has a foreground and a background task. Whatever task is brought to the foreground gets processed—and only that task. "Cooperative multitasking" used to be in Mac computers. Background tasks were only processed when foreground tasks were idle. In current operating systems, "time-slice multitasking" are assigned priority levels but processed in sequential order.

Yes, you read correctly. Computers do not multitask in the strict sense of the term. They are sequential taskers. It may seem like multitasking to the user, but according to the *Computer Dictionary*, this is only because the user's sense of time is much slower than the process-ing speed of the computer. It seems like it is multitasking because our human brain is so much slower.

Nevertheless, I am sure someone is asking, "But what about dual processors? Don't they multitask?" True, many computers now have "multi-core" processors, which is a single computer with two or more independent processors doing their own thing. A "dual-core" proces-sor is what most of us still have at home. It is like having two comput-ers in one case. Soon three or more core will be the norm. While it appears that multi-core computers can run faster, in most applications they do not really run that much faster unless programmers invest a prohibitive amount of time and money in programming them.[7] In addition, the computer cannot think for itself like the human brain can, and every tiny computer step can take a lot of programming. Dual processors may also have to use the same memory and system bus, thus further limiting their real-world performance. In any case, while our brain is only a single processor, it can think for itself and literally program itself on the run. We would need a second skull and brain to mimic a dual processor.

It appears that while computers have some resemblance to the human brain, trying to mimic them or make direct comparisons is not appropriate. The human brain is not just a computer. It is a liv-ing, thinking thing.

Human Limitations in Multitasking

Yes, humans can attend to several things at once. We can drive on a busy street and listen to music at the same time, with only a little risk of being distracted and having an accident. We can shell peas while talking to our spouse, and even keep one eye on the television while carrying on a conversation. However, do not be surprised if your spouse complains that you are not paying attention. But these are not the multitasks that concern us here. Yes, you can drive a car on a busy street while listening to the radio, but we now know that having a conversation on your cell phone while driving is dangerous. What makes the difference? It seems that talking engages and distracts your brain more than just listening to music. It is the degree of chal-lenge or distraction that determines whether you can multitask, not how smart you are. For example, if you are driving a car while trying to text a message on your smartphone, you are a danger to others, and you are breaking the law. We now know that real multitasking is distracting and dangerous.

I (Dr. Hart) can give a perfect example of how intrusive multitasking can be from an encounter with one of my grandchildren. While paying a visit I found my granddaughter sitting on the couch in the family room. She had a computer on her lap and was watching a movie on the large television screen. As I got nearer, I noticed earpieces neatly nesting in each ear, and the computer screen was split in two. In effect, she was watching a movie on television, listening to music in the left ear, the cell phone was in the right ear while conversing with a friend, and she was sending an email on the left side of the computer screen while the right side of the screen was being used to write an essay for her school homework.

I watched for a short while and then opened up a conversation that gently suggested I was quite surprised that she was capable of doing her homework despite the other distractions. Without a pause, she responded: "Papa, if it wasn't for these other things, I wouldn't be able to do my homework. The homework is so dull that I can't stand it. So I do these other things just to keep me here doing my homework."

It was quite an eye-opener. She was correct on several points. First, learning can sometimes be dull. OK, so maybe it's always dull! Some students enjoy writing essays, some don't. I never did. But we don't write essays for enjoyment; we write them so we can learn to express ourselves in writing. Second, it is becoming very common for our youth to engage simultaneously with some other, more pleasant task, or tasks, while doing homework that is dull. Having a friend text a message keeps the dullness away. But, and it is a very big BUT, very little learning can take place in multitasking enjoinment. Brain scientists are very clear on this point: the brain functions best when it only has one task to process at a time. Unfortunately, this message isn't getting through to our youth.

Why Is Multitasking Such a Challenge?

In a sense, we are all multitaskers to some extent. We can walk, talk on our smartphone, chew gum, wave to a friend across the street, and check what time it is, all at once. However, as we have explained, this is not what today's multitasking challenge is all about. These relatively unimportant tasks are not challenging or very distracting, and certainly do not require much brainpower. The modern multitasking we see all around us is far more demanding and intrusive than this.

One explanation for why multitasking is less efficient is that our "memory neurons" become confused and overloaded when we multitask. Switching them on and off, as we do when we multitask, overloads the memory system. This is how it works: let us assume you are a computer programmer working on a complex project. You are deeply engaged in writing some complex computer code but your computer alerts you that a new email has just arrived. You think it might be important, so you set your programming task aside and tackle the email. It is your boss and he wants some information—urgently. You go to the files on your computer, and search high and low. It's not on this computer, so you try again on another computer. Finally, you find what the boss wants and email the information back to him.

You return to your programming task and, having just started, the telephone rings. Another distraction. Then you get back to your programming and have some code laid out. But now you can't remember how you got to where you are. So you have to back up to an earlier and more familiar point in the program and try to pick up where you left off. Problem is, you have wasted half an hour, and this is a rush job! Your stress level goes up, and suddenly you feel like your brain isn't working as well as it did when you were relaxed and only had one thing on your mind.

What is happening here? By jumping from one task to another, you have confused your brain. When you started programming, your brain had assigned a certain section of its memory for the task. These assigned "memory neurons" are there to help you remember where you leave off if you get distracted, and make it easy for you to get back to the task where you left off. Things would have gone fine if you merely answered the email and returned to the task at hand, but the distraction of having to perform another task, before the first was completed, has confused the first group of memory neurons, robbing them of the continuity information that they provide. So, you were not able to go right back to your last programming point, but had to go back to an earlier point. This has interrupted your performance, slowing you down as it always does when you multitask complex activities. If you had only had a minor distraction, your memory neurons would have remembered where you had left off and connected you straight back to that point.

This is why jumping from one task to another, and then another, and then trying to go back to where you left off robs you of performance. On the positive side, you might not feel as bored as you usually do, because frustrations like this can be somewhat stimulating. But progress is slower, not faster, when multitasking. This is the main reason why sequential tasking is preferable to multitasking. You may have to put up with some boredom, but your brain will thrive on it.

There is overwhelming evidence that multitasking lowers our level of performance. Studies at Harvard and Stanford Universities, using their brightest students, support this finding. Giving them sequential and multitasking projects, they found that ALL the students' performances were reduced about one-third when multitasking.[8] What is also notable about this study is that the students ALL reported at the end that they thought they were actually doing better when multitasking than when sequential tasking. Some scientists have likened this to what we see in drunk drivers. They always believe that they are driving well, when in fact they are driving recklessly. Sherry Turkle, MIT professor, says this about multitasking:

> I teach the most brilliant students in the world, but they have done themselves a disservice by drinking the Kool-Aid and believing that a multitasking learning environment will serve their best purposes. There really are important things you cannot think about unless it's still and you are only thinking about one thing at a time. There are just some things that are not amenable to be thought about in conjunction with fifteen other things.[9]

While the myth of multitasking has overtaken a large segment of our education and business world, it might be important for the reader to know that a world of extremely dangerous and demanding tasks has not embraced multitasking. For instance, the Top Gun fighter pilot training program of the United States Navy does not welcome multitaskers as fighter pilots. Fred Harburg, an instructor pilot says, "Good pilots are NOT multitaskers." For this reason, NASA scientists have concluded it is deadly for a pilot to split his or her attention while flying. The best pilots are those who are good at sequencing, not splitting attention.[10]

Other studies have also discovered that multitasking can actually reduce your working intelligence. Just adding a single project to your workload is profoundly debilitating, causing you to lose 20 percent of your time. If you add a third task, nearly half your time is wasted in task switching.[11] This same study, conducted by the Institute of Psychiatry in London, found that excessive use of technology also reduces workers' intelligence. Those distracted by incoming email and phone calls suffered a 10 percent decrease in their working IQ.

With all this research evidence debunking the myth of multitasking, you can't help wondering why it is being ignored in both education and business. If you want to get some idea of how much you or your family members multitask, a simple test is provided in the sidebar.

Multitasking and Learning

The consequences of multitasking are not restricted to the workplace. It affects our ability to learn as well. Studies of Internet users have long shown that websites turn readers into "skimmers." The digital world may offer some learning benefits, but it has also created a learning vacuum. The idea that technology can augment and facilitate learning, as many educators believe, is over-stated and misleading. Is there a "dumbing down" effect when it comes to learning? I (Dr. Hart), as a professor of psychology for the past forty years, believe there is. Internet overuse is making our students shallow thinkers, as some experts allege.[12]

The effect of multitasking on the brain is still being studied. Brain scans of long-term multitaskers show that there is increased flow of blood to one part of the frontal brain called "Brodmann Area 10" (see figure 1).

This part of the brain has been referred to as "It's what makes us human." What researchers have found is that whenever task switching occurs, as in multitasking, there is a "response selections bottleneck." Time is lost because the brain is trying to sort out which task to perform at a time when several tasks need to be performed. They have also found that multitasking contributes to the release of stress hormones such as adrenaline, which in excessive amounts can cause long-term health problems.[13] It also leads to a loss of short-term memory and could seriously affect our learning ability.

Some experts have taken an optimistic view of multitasking's impact on learning by suggesting that with training, the brain can learn to task-switch more effectively. While this may be true for simple multiple tasks, the growing body of evidence shows that "even if

Test for Multitasking Addiction

Definition: The term *multitasking* means engaging in multiple activities or sources of stimulation, like MP3 players, iPods, iTunes, computer messaging, Googling and searching, or other computer music players, AT THE SAME TIME.

Instructions: While a teenager can take this test, the problem is that he or she might downplay the seriousness of the problem. Therefore, we recommend that you take the test yourself and assess how you are doing and then take it as applied to the teenager in your life.

To assess your teenager's level of addiction to multitasking, give a score using the following ratings to each of the questions:

0 for—Never or rarely

1 for—Occasionally (seems to be able to control it)

2 for—Often (several times a week, but for a long time)

3 for—Always (every day, and for a lot of the time)

SCORE

_____ 1. Your teenager neglects household chores in order to multitask.

_____ 2. He/she prefers the excitement of being stimulated by multiple tasks more than going out to play or be with friends.

_____ 3. You have to cajole your teenager to stop a computer game or activity in order to come to dinner or a family activity.

_____ 4. Your teenager's interactions with friends are mainly via the Internet.

_____ 5. Spending time multitasking is clearly having a detrimental effect on your teenager's grades.

_____ 6. The time spent multitasking is clearly having a detrimental effect on your teenager's relationships with friends and family.

_____ 7. Your teenager loses sleep because he or she spends time multitasking.

_____ 8. Your teenager appears depressed or moody, but cheers up when multitasking.

_____ 9. When the means for multitasking is not available (computer down, cell phone or "gadget" not working, etc.), your teenager becomes moody or angry.

_____ 10. Your teenager appears unable really to enjoy anything that does not involve multitasking.

_____ TOTAL SCORE

Interpreting the score:

10 or less: Your teenager does not appear to be addicted to multitasking and is able to exercise appropriate control.

11 to 14: Your teenager may be experiencing occasional dependence on multitasking and may be showing signs of a growing addiction.

15 to 17: Your teenager's use of multitasking is excessive, addiction will become evident, and the problem needs to be addressed with some degree of urgency.

18 to 20: Your teenager is clearly addicted to multitasking and needs professional help.

Figure 1
"Brodmann Area 10" in the Human Brain

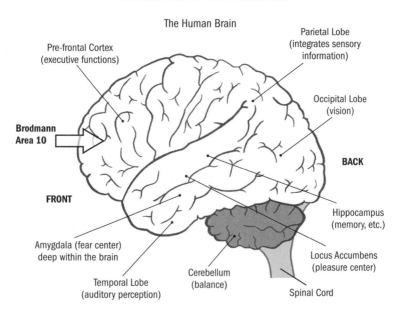

The Human Brain

Pre-frontal Cortex
(executive functions)

Parietal Lobe
(integrates sensory
information)

Occipital Lobe
(vision)

**Brodmann
Area 10**

BACK

FRONT

Hippocampus
(memory, etc.)

Amygdala (fear center)
deep within the brain

Locus Accumbens
(pleasure center)

Cerebellum
(balance)

Temporal Lobe
(auditory perception)

Spinal Cord

you learn while multitasking, that learning is less flexible and more specialized, so you cannot retrieve information as easily."[14]

This throws a wrench in the works for many educators who were relying on educating our kids to become better multitaskers. Psychologists and neurologists are insistent that there is a cost to the way our society is changing. Humans are not built to function this way. And these are not even Christians trying to preserve our belief in how God has created us. Dr. Poldrack, a prominent psychologist from the University of California, Los Angeles, who has researched this area extensively, made the following statement in a National Public Radio broadcast:

> We're really built to focus. And when we sort of force ourselves to multitask, we're driving ourselves to perhaps be less efficient in the long run even though it sometimes feels like we're being more efficient. . . . Multitasking changes the way people learn.[15]

We've taken quite a bit of space here to make the point that parents need to be more intentional in guiding their children through their digital challenges and not uncritically embrace the value of multi-tasking. We live in an era when we are more hurried, hassled, and agitated than ever before. This applies to our children as much as it does to us adults. Yes, there have been other times in history when changes have bothered us, but no change in all of history has been more intrusive and disruptive as the change we are now seeing in our modern digital world. Dr. Edward Hallowell, a psychiatrist, expresses it this way: "Never in history has the human brain been asked to track so many data points. This challenge can only be controlled by creatively engineering one's environment and one's emotional and physical health."[16] Limiting multitasking is essential, according to Dr. Hallowell. Some dos and don'ts for parents of multitasking teenagers are provided in the next sidebar.

Multitasking and "Attention Deficit Trait"

As we have tried to show, there is a growing consensus that multi-tasking is a poor long-term strategy for learning. But a more serious aspect has recently emerged. Multitasking robs us of the ability to pay attention. As every parent and teacher knows, paying attention is essential to learning. People who have accomplished great things all have one essential characteristic: they have mastered the art of paying attention. Sir Isaac Newton, who some consider to be the greatest scientist who ever lived, attributed his discoveries, like gravity and the three laws of motion, to his finely tuned ability to pay attention. He was also a Christian believer who saw God as the Master Creator and whose existence could not be denied. He was correct on another point: he believed there had to be "a transition from youthful distraction to mature attention" in everyone's life. In other words, it is natural for the very young to be distractible. But as a child matures, he or she has to learn how to stay focused and pay attention, and this only happens through disciplined training, not multitasking. What is unfortunate about our digital world is that unless its use is disciplined, where parents take control of their children's digital world, it can never deliver the level of attention that maturity demands.

This is why Dr. Hallowell has proposed the idea that the distraction of trying to perform two or more tasks simultaneously can lead to a condition called "Attention Deficit Trait."[17] In many respects, it

Dos and Don'ts for Parents of Multitasking Teenagers

Don't

- Condemn any behavior you haven't taken the trouble to understand yourself.
- Expect your child to do less multitasking when you are overdoing it yourself.
- Give in to your teenager's temper tantrums, pouting, or bad-mouthing.
- Label your teenager as "bad" or use "love withdrawal" to condemn behavior. They are always entitled to your respect and unconditional love.
- Let technology intimidate you. Some parents don't set limits because they are embarrassed and afraid it will show up their ignorance.

Do

- Experiment with the Internet yourself, as this will increase your credibility to set limits.
- Monitor all multitasking activities (listening to music, doing homework, and texting) and try to limit the number to as few as possible, preferably only one at a time.
- Try reinforcing behavior that focuses on single activities, like just doing their homework or just watching television. Praise it, and reward it.
- Set clear limits as to both the time and intensity of all activities that are stimulating.
- Encourage relaxation, taking time out, going outside, and changing their immediate environment.
- Foster as much physical activity as you can, as this counteracts the high level of stimulation by helping the body to burn off excess adrenaline.
- Make sure you have set up a "protection" program that limits access to certain undesirable websites.

simulates true Attention Deficit Disorder (ADD). He sees this trait not only as rampant in the business world, where workers are called on to perform multiple tasks all the time, but it may partially account for the epidemic we are now seeing in ADD among children and possibly adults. They may not be suffering from the classic form of ADD but from an enforced lack of adequate attention caused by the multitasking phenomenon. We believe that all this wealth of information is creating a poverty of attention.

Teaching Our Children to "Pay Attention"

Given that multitasking can dramatically reduce attention, especially among our children and young adults, we want to offer some practical help for parents. We anticipate that in the not-too-distant future we might even see the emergence of smartphone apps that are designed to improve the attention spans of our youth, a sort of "paying attention" app. If technology is as clever as it purports to be, then surely it can come up with effective attention-building tools. It's very feasible that devices that detect the moment you are being distracted can be devised. They can then alert you and call you back to what you should be focusing on. Some serious research in this area is already under way.

But until technology comes up with a solution to our distractibility, here are some old-fashioned parenting strategies you can follow:

- Start by modeling staying focused on a particular task yourself. Make sure you do so in the presence of your children, and encourage them to join with you in the experience. For example, working on a painting and identifying its key features. Or get a book for your children and one for yourself. Start by reading to your children before they go to bed so that they can acquire a taste for interesting children's books. Later, invite your children to sit with you so you can all read together. While reading alone can be boring for a child, reading with someone else can be quite pleasurable.

- Since physical movement stimulates the brain by increasing blood circulation and stimulating our energy hormones, don't let your children spend long periods of time just sitting, even if it is reading a book. Intermix inactivity with physical activity. For every minute spent being inactive, your family needs to spend a minute in activity. Take hikes, ride bicycles, or just do physical activities around the house. Your body and brain need oxygen to function well, and the only way you can boost it is with physical movement.

- Activities that require hand/eye coordination, like crafts or model building, can also be helpful. It keeps your child focused, as do puzzles and games like Chess, Scrabble, and Boggle. Planting and caring for a garden is also extremely helpful. My (Dr. Hart's) tomato garden has just started to blossom. Caring for it takes me outdoors for a period every day and is highly pleasurable.

Give each of your children a piece of your yard to plant whatever they want and then see that they take care of it.

- Allow your children to help you in the kitchen. Boy or girl, teach them how to cook and allow them to find and cook a recipe of their choosing. When I was twelve years old, my grandmother started teaching me how to cook. She had a German background, so she taught me to cook many traditional dishes. Sauerbraten was my favorite, and to this day I bless her for taking the time to teach me this skill.

- When buying a toy for your child, try to get one that requires some assembly and skill building. Toys that require some assembly can be more enjoyable than others, because one learns to build and repair things, and it can help to build focus. So, instead of buying a bicycle fully assembled, buy one that needs assembly, and then let your child help while you struggle to find out what goes where. It will be a memory that is cherished, even if it is a little challenging. It also builds skills they will take pleasure in all their life.

- Finally, keep your frustration to a minimum. Don't expect perfect cooperation from your children, and never use any form of punishment when there is noncompliance. The goal is to make activities that build attention. If you lose your temper, you create fear. There will be slips, but pick up where you left off and keep going again.

Effective Cyber Learning

We recently came across an article offering help to teens who multitask on an iPhone or iPod. These gadgets are constant companions to children on their way to school riding in the back of Mom's car or on a school bus or even just walking to school. Newer smartphones are intuitive and allow users to open many apps at the same time, and on the face of it, it seems innocuous. Some see it as helpful in training children to multitask. They can talk to a friend on the phone, answer a short message, switch back to a suspended game they were playing earlier, and then go back to their friend's conversation. Supposedly, this makes your children better multitaskers. Manuals offer training in how to do this switching, though we suspect that every digital native knows how to do it intuitively. The technologists who design these systems know what they are doing and they take advantage of the digital native's adaptability. After all, it does sell smartphones.

What We Can Do about It

Uni-tasking and single tasking is the solution. We can learn how to uni-task—doing one thing at a time. It will allow the brain to work faster and more efficiently. It is up to you as the parent to decide which app and game is an effective tool in your child's learning. Instill in your children the value of doing just one task at a time.

Simplify your environment. Our brain is programmed to pay attention to new stimuli. When you are at your computer, close the windows you aren't using, turn off Twitter, and disable automatic email notification. Put unnecessary papers out of sight, and turn off your cell phone's ringer. Work on building your focus. Chronic multitaskers weaken their ability to focus.

Set aside some time, even if it's just five minutes, to deal with a mentally challenging task; once you accomplish that, extend the time further. Embrace the discomfort that comes from doing a difficult

---

Five Free Apps That Can Help You Reclaim Your Time
(Just Google and download them)

1. *Rescue Time*—This app is designed to help you cut down time spent on social media sites. At the end of a week receive a printout of a complete analysis of time spent. This will make you aware of where your time goes.
2. *Easy Task Manager*—Helps you to prioritize, strategize, and get things crossed off your list. For Macs only.
3. *Think*—Helps you cut down on multitasking. Blocks everything except the program you are working on. For Macs only.
4. *Stay Focused*—Instead of tracking your time, this app limits the time you spend on social media sites. You can program it so you can spend, say, 60 minutes on Facebook, then it logs you off when your time is up.
5. *Focus Booster*—This app will break your tasks into 30-minute increments and sound an alarm every 25 minutes for you to take a 5-minute break.

task and try not to escape to something easier. Any project you do that requires mental effort, or involves critical thinking and creativity, is going to be a little painful sometimes. Try to push through when you hit a wall.

Work on taking breaks, because humans work in cycles; we can concentrate for a period of time but then need time to rest. Every hour or so, take a quick walk around the block, or just step away from your desk for a few minutes.

Our hope is that you and your family become smarter by controlling your multitasking and then spread the news that doing one thing at a time is a mark of true intelligence.

Discussion Questions

1. Discuss your thoughts about the idea that "*not* multitasking is a mark of intelligence."

2. How have you seen multitasking affecting your productivity—at home and at work?

3. Discuss the differences between multitasking and sequential tasking.

4. Think of ways that you can limit the amount of multitasking you do.

5. What would it look like for you to try to master, like Sir Isaac Newton, the art of paying attention?

6. How did you score on the "Test for Multitasking Addiction"? What changes do you think you need to make in your life or work?

5

Relationships and Social Media

Authentic connection is described as the core of psychological well-being and is the essential quality of growth fostering and healing relationships.[1]

Janet L. Surrey

A recent news magazine report carried a most illuminating description of how one of their journalists spent a week on vacation. She was determined to try to break an addiction to social networking she had developed over the past two years. Writing about her experience, she describes how she was constantly tweeting on her two smartphones. She persistently wanted to share her everyday experiences with her friends. Sometimes she connected to Facebook, sometimes to LinkedIn. It could be a Twitter feed if she was hurried, or YouTube if she had a video to share. Staying connected had become an obsession, and she was wise enough to admit it.

Recently she had begun to realize what an obnoxious dining companion she'd become. When one friend described her as a "social-media addict," that took it to a whole new level. She realized that she had crossed a boundary she had never even thought of setting up. Just how often and for how long should one digitally connect for socialization? She came to realize that socializing one-on-one and face-to-face is a lot healthier than the superficial tweet, text, or email. So, when she was due to take a five-day vacation that was intended to give her some relaxation and recovery time, she decided she would disconnect completely from all electronic communication and focus on what really was in front of her. She vowed to rid herself from her addiction while she was on this trip, and establish healthier boundaries. It was quite an eye-opener, and she chronicled the whole experience.

It was not an easy challenge. She knew that her addiction wouldn't just go away. She would need to be on guard and intentional in resisting the temptation to tweet everyone about her moment-by-moment holiday experience. To resist any temptation, she locked her two smartphones in her hotel room's safe. A friend, who had gone through a similar experience, had warned her that it would be difficult at first, but she would start to enjoy being disconnected fairly quickly.

Her basic struggle boiled down to this: she always wanted to share what she was experiencing by tweeting. She felt compelled to include others in her experience. As she persisted in keeping her experience to herself, she slowly began to realize how much more fulfilling it was as a private experience. It was much more gratifying if she just relished it and stayed in the moment. To her delight, by the fourth day of her vacation, she no longer felt the urge to share every experience, but enjoyed it for herself.

We Are Created for Connection

The social media problem we want to confront is not only highly addicting and difficult to break out of, as evidenced by this journalist's experience. But the digital social media phenomena can have a deeper effect on us.

God has created us for authentic connection and meaningful attachments—the kind of connection that has the power to secure, grow, free and transform us. Psychologist Janet L. Surrey expresses it well: "In moments of deep connection in our relationships, we break out of isolation and contraction into a more whole and spacious state of mind and heart."[2] Research shows that human connection is one of the keys to happiness. Connections are what make us human and are the core of how we express our humanity. The question we face here is this: can all the connecting done through the social media of our digital world provide us with the lasting connections we need to be fulfilled and secure? Technology can help us connect with extended relationships, but it also disconnects us from our most intimate relationships. We turn to technology for connections we can control, like texting, tweeting, emailing, and posting. These allow us to edit, delete, and retouch what we say and how we look. Real conversations are hard work, messy, challenging, unpredictable, and time consuming, but they are worth it.

It would be an exaggeration to assume that the journalist we described above could totally overcome her social media addiction simply by setting up a smartphone moratorium on her five-day holiday. She acknowledges in her article that it will take a lot more transformation than this. But for her it was a good start. She returned to work at the end of her short vacation and reconnected face-to-face with her friends. She describes herself as now being a better listener and more able to give others her undivided attention. She came to realize that there are always two sides to every relationship, and every healthy social alliance has to contribute equally to the relationship. Unfortunately, the digital social media that now dominates our lives tends to foster more self-centeredness than deeper connections.

The Narcissism Epidemic

This journalist's experience also highlights one of the major drawbacks of our overuse of social media, namely, that it fosters the growth of narcissism, which is now seen as epidemic in our young people. For those readers who are not familiar with the concept of narcissism, it is a term that describes a person who has an inflated or grandiose sense of self. Narcissists are preoccupied with themselves and are obsessed with what others think of them. They also believe that they are entitled to the attention of everyone else.

What has narcissism got to do with social media? It appears to be a major consequence of excessive media connections. The extreme use of social media does not promote more concern or care of others. Rather, it facilitates a focusing on oneself, seeing oneself as the center of the universe. Narcissists are not particularly interested in, or good at offering, warmth and caring in their social interactions. They can enjoy being around people and can be most charming, flattering, and likable. But it is all for their own benefit.

How do we know there is a growing epidemic of narcissism, especially in our youth? The evidence comes from three sources: the dramatic growth in the use of social media, changes that are taking place in our youth, and changes taking place in our culture. The growth of narcissism is well documented in a book by Jean Twenge and W. Keith Campbell entitled *The Narcissism Epidemic*. In it they say, "The name 'MySpace' is no coincidence. The slogan of 'YouTube' is 'Broadcast Yourself.' The name 'Facebook' is just right, with its nuance of seeing and being seen, preferably looking as attractive as possible."[3]

Social networking is not a challenge just for the digital natives of our world. It is growing by leaps and bounds in the digital immigrant world as well. When emailing arrived in the early history of the Internet, it revolutionized our communication and had only a slight effect on our relationships. But the "New Email," as some have called it, has outstripped the old emailing. The statistics below reveal the huge black hole that our time disappears into when we visit Facebook, Twitter, YouTube, or other social media sites.

• One in every nine people on Earth is on Facebook.

• People spend 700 billion minutes per month on Facebook.

• YouTube has 490 million unique users who visit every month.

• Wikipedia hosts 17 million articles.

• People upload 3,000 images to Flickr (the photo sharing social media site) every minute.

• 190 million average tweets per day occur on Twitter.[4]

Although Internet communication is more public than many other modes of communication, according to psychologist John Suler there is a tendency called "the online disinhibition effect" where people engaged in online interaction "loosen up, feel less restrained, and express themselves more openly." Suler goes on to say, "While online, some people self-disclose or act out more frequently or intensely than they would in person."[5] Somehow they think that what they are doing is anonymous, so they lower their guard and say things they believe will be kept private.

The problem with the digital world is that it is not private, nor does it forget. It's like getting a tattoo. If you have Facebooked it, downloaded it, or posted it, there is a record of it floating out there in cyberspace. It is crucial to remember that anything posted online may stay there forever, in some form or another. That means every post and every picture you upload or download could be evaluated and judged. This is a good reminder that we all need to be good stewards of our digital, virtual life. The virtual world is watching!

Why Do We Expect More from Technology and Less from Each Other?

As of February 2013, Facebook has more than one billion active users. Users must register before using the site, after which they can create a personal profile, add other users as friends, and exchange messages, including automatic notifications when they update their profile. Facebook is surpassing telephones, cell phones, and email as an easy and more natural way of communication between friends. Too much dependence on technology also creates new social problems as people become socially withdrawn, disliking real-life meetings, avoiding working in teams, and fearing face-to-face contact and preferring online communication instead. This explains why the social networks have experienced exponential growth these last few years. So their virtual life connects them on the one hand and separates them on the other.

Our traditional understanding of friendship is that of a relationship between two people, where that relationship requires us to give something of ourselves to each other. We spend time with our friends, we invest ourselves (emotionally, psychologically, and even financially) in our friends, and we reciprocate by listening to what they want to share. But relationships with Facebook friends usually do not include these more personal exchanges. In some cases, we don't even interact with a Facebook friend at all, since it's not unusual for a regular Facebooker to have several hundred "friends." When we do interact, our interactions are mainly superficial and impersonal, and lack any of the deep emotional investments we find in our real friendships outside of our virtual life. To put it in a nutshell, for the most part, Facebook friendships make no demands of us.

MIT social psychologist Sherry Turkle believes that through our overuse of social media, we have come to expect more from technology and less from each other. She states:

> Overwhelmed by the volume and velocity of our lives, we turn to technology to help us find time. But technology makes us busier than ever, and ever more in search of retreat. Gradually, we come to see our online life as life itself.[6]

Dr. Turkle goes on to say that instead of learning how to handle the give-and-take of real conversation, we craft and edit witty text responses. She explains that when we communicate through text messages, our communication is much more limited than when we communicate in person. Talking online or through texts excludes the communication of body language, voice inflections, and eye contact. You don't see the tears or feel the pain that only the face can show. This means that the less face-to-face communication you have with people, the worse your real social skills will probably become.

With the growing decline in social skills, we really have to ask ourselves, what long-term effects will our socializing in the digital world have on our deeper relationships? More specifically, are teens and young adults who depend heavily on social media contacts developing healthy relationship skills and the emotional intelligence needed to sustain, say, a happy marriage? Are parents maintaining the social and emotional skills necessary to communicate with each other and with their children? We are already abbreviating deep emotional terms in our texting, to the extent that they no longer communicate our deeper feelings. This could be detrimental to healthy attachment and relationship building. As an example, our texting uses digital acronyms, saying things like LOL (laughing out loud), IMY (I miss you) and WYWH (wish you were here). Sorry, but we just don't get the same emotional response from such abbreviations as we do when someone says them face-to-face. It feels like the sender doesn't have the time, or courage, to speak the real words of deep feelings. This stunts emotional and social development. One teenager insightfully described it like this:

> Lots of my friends are more comfortable texting than they are talking and having real relationships. They have trouble with face-to-face intimacy because they're so used to living with their lives online and in text messages. Texting feels safer than telling someone face to face what you feel.

Yes, texting does feel safer. Because you don't really have to say what you really feel, you find this a safe hiding place. Technology may be a speedy way to transmit information, but it cannot convey deep, underlying nonverbal modes of communication.

A good rule of thumb for yourself, and to teach to your children, is to use the digital world to relay necessary information, but communicate deeper thoughts and emotions in direct face-to-face encounters. This is essential in today's digital world for laying the foundation of healthy connections and relationships.

Twelve Ways to Improve Communication

1. Relax
2. Stay present
3. Cultivate inner silence
4. Increase positivity
5. Reflect on your deepest values
6. Access a pleasant memory
7. Observe nonverbal cues
8. Express appreciation
9. Speak warmly
10. Speak slowly
11. Speak briefly
12. Listen deeply

Rise of Online Dating

One of the significant ways social media technology is changing our world is in how we date. With the enormous growth of socializing online, it makes sense that many people have gone to the Internet to search for their ideal "soul mate." Online dating services are growing in number, even in the Christian believer's world, and there is no doubt they serve a purpose. One dating website claims that they are responsible for nearly 5 percent of marriages in the US.[7] And their numbers are growing.

But there are important questions that need clarification: Is online dating equivalent to, or different from conventional dating? Does it promote a better romantic outcome?

A recent *Association for Psychological Science* report states that while communicating online can foster intimacy and affection between strangers, it can also lead to unrealistic expectations and disappointment when potential partners finally meet in person. Although many dating sites tout the superiority of their partner matching service, claiming that they use "scientific algorithms" for predictively matching partners, there is little evidence that these algorithms can always predict whether two people are good matches or not. You can't create the "chemistry of love" that is needed for early dating by merely matching people on a number of characteristics. The report goes on to state:

> The existing matching algorithms neglect the most important insights from the flourishing discipline of relationship science. The algorithms

seek to predict long-term romantic compatibility from characteristics of the two partners before they meet. Yet the strongest predictors of relationship well-being, such as a couple's interaction style and ability to navigate stressful circumstances, cannot be assessed with such data.[8]

While we do not want to discourage online dating, we do want to emphasize that only real time spent with someone, in a variety of situations, will reveal all aspects of the true person. This means that however careful one is in choosing a partner, it is not enough to just find a good "starting match." In fact, there is no such thing as a perfect "match." Marriage is more about "becoming" the right person than in "finding" the right person. Every marriage demands a lot of readjusting, which mainly happens after you are married and living with one another. That is when the real work of "matching" begins. No matter how closely you are matched, by whatever criteria devised, taking the time to get to know someone and start this "becoming" stage with lots of in-person contact and communication is the key to a good marriage.

Being Smart about Online Dating

1. Stay in control.
2. Protect personal details.
3. Ask for a recent photo.
4. Meet for the first time in a safe place.
5. Use a paid online dating service.
6. Keep your friend in the know.
7. Common sense rules.[9]

A Lonely Future?

Another serious concern about how digital social media is affecting our relationships is our vulnerability to what some have called "emotional contagion." For instance, research by John Cacioppo and his colleagues at the University of Chicago has shown that *loneliness* can be transmitted via social networks.[10] Positive and negative emotions can spread quickly "like the flu and anyone can catch it." Cacioppo's findings suggest that if someone you have direct social connection with is lonely, you are 52 percent more likely to become lonely too. In other words, these emotions are contagious. If the connection is a friend of a friend, you are 25 percent more likely to feel lonely. If the connection is a distant contact, like a friend of a friend of a friend, there is a 15 percent risk for feeling lonely.

But the contagion is not confined to one emotion. The phenomenon also means that if someone in your online social network is angry or hostile, and takes it out on you, they are more likely to transmit these moods to you. So, even though you may never have met this person or interacted with them in real life, their "bad behavior" can still influence yours. This has significant implications for our children, who could have many digital contacts. We need to be on guard against developing negative contagions by selecting our friends carefully and "de-friending" those who are having a negative effect on our children or on us.

Current research also reveals that digital natives who spend most of their time in a virtual world will more likely be lonely. It is not surprising, therefore, that we have seen an increase in the incidence of isolation and loneliness in the young at a time when social media is on the rise. Too many people lock themselves into "virtual living," rather than interact with others in real-life circumstances.

Nevertheless, this raises an interesting question: How is it possible for a person who has 700 Facebook friends to feel lonely and isolated? The answer is not so difficult to discern. First, one cannot be a "real" friend to 700 "virtual" friends. The fact is, if you only had five real friends, you probably would be a lot happier. Second, Facebook can be misleading. It can make a user think that his or her virtual friend is happier than him or her. This distortion makes people feel lonely and dissatisfied with life.

Because the inappropriate use of social media is increasingly becoming a challenge, we want to offer some guidelines for you and your family so you can become more sociable and deal with loneliness without depending on social media programs:

5 TIPS FOR OVERCOMING LONELINESS

1. *Get honest with your feelings*. Ask yourself, am I really alone here? You may be surrounded by friends, acquaintances, and family members who love you. Most of us aren't truly alone but maybe are lacking a confidant or best friend.

2. *Take responsibility for your loneliness*. Assess what you have done to create friendships, try to meet new people, and put yourself out there. If that isn't working, review what approach you've been using and ask yourself why it isn't working. Are

you trying to make friends with people who don't share the same interests? Have you been pursuing someone who is too busy and doesn't have time?

3. *Find your passion.* One of the best ways to meet like-minded people is to get out and do the things that you love. When people are doing what they love, they are generally happy and emitting a positive energy that attracts others to them.

4. *Show consistency.* To meet new people, join a small group at your church and just keep showing up. Also try to frequent the same places at the same times. When you go to church, go at the same time and sit in the same general area. Go to the same gym class each week. Being familiar with others who have the same routine is an easy way to make connections.

5. *If you want a friend, be a friend.* The old adage still rings true. Reach out to those around you and work on being the kind of friend you would like to have. Try allowing people into your life that reach out to you as well.

Facebook and Twitter Comparisons

It used to be that all we had to worry about was trying to keep up with the "Joneses" next door. Now with Facebook, Twitter, and the like, we have thousands of "Joneses" to keep up with. And none of us is immune to the posts and tweets that leave us comparing and contrasting our lives with others. We have all read our friends' postings about being married to the most amazing wife or husband or how they have the best kids in the world. Those pictures posted from our friends' dream trip to Hawaii, their job promotions, pictures of their new cars, and the like, can leave us all feeling that we are missing out on life. The feeling that one is missing out on life is quite common in Facebook users and is known as "Facebook facade." Only the acceptable, successful, and presentable facades are posted, so one is left with the impression that everyone else has an amazing life, except for me.

Let's take one young mom, Susie, as an example of how Facebook caused her to compare her daughter with her friend's daughter. Susie took her daughter to the doctor to find out what was wrong with her. She had read on Facebook how her friend's daughter was already reading well at four years of age, while her own daughter, the same age, was not reading at all. Then there is Jeff. Reading the posts on Facebook, he finds that his friend's wife is making very complimentary comments about her husband, his friend, and feels envious because his wife doesn't make posts like that about him. These and many other examples illustrate how social media can create a "comparison trap." One gets pulled into constantly making comparisons, contrasting your own life or children's lives with others, and in the process, diminishing what you perceive to be the quality of your own life. Social media tools can quickly change relationships by turning our friends into an audience and us into the performers.

You can avoid this self-judging trap by practicing gratitude. Be thankful for who God has made you and your family to be. Practice the art of contentment, for who you are and what you have. Comparing yourself and your family with others will always cause dissatisfaction and steal the joy and happiness you should be experiencing and place it just outside of your reach.

My (Dr. Frejd's) daughter recently saw this posted on a girl's dorm room at her college:

> You are much more interesting than your profile, much more attractive than your pics. So get off Facebook and enjoy real life with someone in person.

Facebook Depression

> Fear is very much part of the climate of Facebook. When we are afraid of what people think of us, we work hard to craft just the right image, composed of just the right pictures, personal information and status updates. The emphasis is on being clever, not on being genuine.[11]

These are the words of Jesse Rice, taken from his book, *The Church of Facebook*.

Studies now show that too much time spent on Facebook and other social networks can cause "Facebook Depression." It is a form of depression that is created by comparing yourself too much with others on Facebook. Keeping up Facebook facades and making comparisons as we have just described can breed a deep sense of discontentment, and these distortions can ultimately trigger a deep depression because you can't live up to the false standards that social media mostly presents. With all the inrush of people's status updates and pictures, it is easy for our successes to feel diminished and our failures amplified. This sense of loss is what can create depression.

I (Dr. Frejd) must make my Facebook confession at this point. Just last week I was surfing on Facebook and noticed that a particular person I had recently "friended" had 2,000 friends. To be honest, it made me feel very insecure, like I didn't measure up. Questions flooded my mind. Why didn't I have more Facebook friends? What was wrong with me that more people haven't friended me? So I started putting in additional friend requests to see how quickly I could build up my account. I know, I know. How could I—especially since I am writing a book on the subject and should know better! I saw firsthand how easy it is to get caught up in the false reality that social media is so good at creating.

Of course, social networking can be a valuable tool for building and maintaining relationships you have already formed, especially if you have friends and family far away or want to contact old friends. But it is not a satisfactory substitute for real, in-person relationships. A new study shows that even though the average user of Facebook has a network of 100 friends, he or she regularly keeps in contact with only a few of them. I (Dr. Frejd) like to tell people they don't have 500 Facebook friends, they have 500 Facebook "contacts." There is a big difference!

So how much time on Facebook is too much? If you're on for more than an hour a day, you may want to evaluate your situation. Whatever you're trying to do on Facebook or in other social media, you should be able to do within an hour. In fact, if you're really focused, you should be able to do your Facebook updates in less than thirty minutes.

Another way to manage your social media is to get rid of the "notification options" from Facebook and Twitter, so you don't feel compelled to check the constant updates. You can deal with them when you have the time. Remember, real life and real people come first. If you make the commitment to yourself that face-to-face interaction and living "in the now" always trumps every other method of communication, you will be on your way to a healthier and more fulfilling life.

Facebook Addiction Disorder

It may come as a surprise, but there is strong evidence that excessive use of social media programs like Facebook can become an addiction. Many, especially teenagers and midlife women, are spending too much time online accessing social media. Social psychologists have come to believe that such an addiction is possible and call it "FAD," or "Face-book Addiction Disorder." They say it is a condition that is defined by long hours spent on Facebook—so much time that the healthy balance of the individual's life is affected. It is estimated that approximately 350 million people are now suffering from this disorder.[12]

According to *Psychology Today*, Facebook and Twitter are more addictive than tobacco and alcohol. In an article by Michael W. Austin in *Ethics for Everyone*, a recent study claims that for some, "quit-ting Facebook (and Twitter) is more difficult than quitting smoking or giving up alcohol."[13] In this study of the everyday desires of 250 people, it was found that what people want most over the course of the day is sex and sleep. However, the urge to stay on top of one's online social networks was the most difficult to resist. In fact, the level of desire for a Facebook encounter for many was higher than that for both alcohol and tobacco.

If these studies are correct, social networking poses a very special menace to those with "addictive" personalities or tendencies. It is well known that being addicted to one behavior or substance can increase your risk of forming another addiction.

Facebook Affairs

This leads us to another important aspect of social media. A recent study shows as many as one in five divorces now involve Facebook affairs.[14] Social networking sites that connect past flames and allow users to make new friends online are to blame for an increasing num-ber of marriages ending.

- 57% of people have used the Internet to flirt.
- 38% of people have engaged in explicit online sexual conversation.
- 50% of people have talked on the phone with someone they first chatted with online.
- 31% of people have had an online conversation that has led to in-person sex.[15]

Thousands of marriages are in trouble this very moment because someone fueled an improper relationship on the Internet. Of course, this isn't the fault of social networking sites, nor of the Internet itself,

Steps to Preventing Facebook Affairs

1. *Keep working at growing in your marriage.* Every marriage is susceptible to boredom, feelings of loneliness, desire for a simpler life, cravings for romance, or just plain old curiosity. Work through a good marriage book, attend a marriage seminar, spend a few hours with a mentor couple, or take a long weekend without the children or work.

2. *Be aware that "It could happen to me."* Place boundaries so that it cannot happen to you. Do NOT flirt! It may boost your ego, but it is not worth it. One woman wrote, "Pay attention to the red flags and pray for strength when they come along. And be willing to hit the 'remove from friends' button if the relationship is moving into the flirting zone."

3. *Status on Facebook.* Set your relationship status to "Married"—bold and clear. Never try to mislead those you connect with on Facebook.

4. *Be honest with your spouse about everything you do on the Internet.* Be honest about who you are friending and communicating with. Openness with your spouse regarding your Facebook is the key. Don't friend ex-boyfriends or ex-girlfriends.

5. *Share user name and passwords with your spouse.* It is very important that you can access each other's accounts for accountability.

6. *Post pictures of your spouse and family on your profile page.* Also post positive comments about them and make your spouse a post topic regularly.

7. *Be honest with yourself about where you are vulnerable and what your intentions are.*

8. *Take drastic action if Facebook is a weakness for you.* You may have to treat it like a porn site. If your propensity for developing Internet relationships could harm your marriage, then delete your account and get professional help.

but these tools make it much easier to get into these situations. Affairs on Facebook and other social networking sites are threatening healthy marriages too. This study also suggests that connecting with old boyfriends or girlfriends on Facebook can also cause a disconnect from your spouse.

As counselors, we (Drs. Frejd and Hart) have seen firsthand the impact that Facebook has had on marriages. Here are a few of the stories of marriages that have been impacted by Facebook so that the reader can understand the risks involved.

It all started out innocently enough for Pete.[16] His high school girl-friend found him on Facebook and posted some pictures from their yearbook of the two of them together. He felt a rush of adrenaline talking with her and it made him feel like a schoolboy again. Soon they were chatting back and forth, flirting like when they were in high school. He justified his actions by telling himself it was all harmless fun. And it was at first. But slowly, and before Pete knew it, he had arranged to meet with her. It wasn't long after this encounter that his wife found out they were having an affair and asked for a divorce.

Brittany, a divorcée, developed an infatuation with a married man she was working with. She added him to her Facebook friends and they started messaging privately. It soon developed into a flirty, sexual "thing." Saying things they wouldn't have said in person, Facebook made it easy to get away with it online. She constantly checked his Facebook status, who he was talking to, what was going on in his life, and where he was going. It became an obsession. She posted things constantly on Facebook to send "messages" to him indirectly. They ended up getting very emotionally entangled, and she became obsessed with him. Soon she developed a jealous streak, and when other women posted anything to him she became jealous and would question him until he became angry. As it turns out, he was also doing the Facebook thing with other women. She eventually found out, came to her senses, and dropped him. But it was extremely painful "de-friending" him, and even more painful to break her addiction and obsession to Facebook.

As we have listened to similar stories about Facebook affairs, we discovered that most victims of these affairs say the same thing: "I don't know how this happened. I thought we were okay. How did I get into this mess?" Clearly, playing affair games like this on social media is a slippery slope; once you start, it is difficult to stop.

The Digital Impact on Marriage

With the dramatic increase in cyber-affairs, we thought that our own homebred marriage expert, Dr. Sharon Hart May,[17] my (Dr. Frejd's) sister and Dr. Hart's daughter, could provide us with some helpful information on how the Internet is impacting marriages in general.

Dr. May believes that the Internet has become more damaging than helpful to marriages. She shared that the Internet distracts couples from spending time together and making emotional and physical connections. These connections are what fuel a marriage. Many of the people who are having emotional affairs through Facebook aren't aware of how damaging this is to their marriage. It becomes a "competing attachment" to their marriage. Sadly, there is no protocol on what your boundaries should be with opposite-sex relationships in social media.

Dr. May has also seen an increase in the accessibility through the Internet to people, products, and places that become hindrances to marriage. There are men and women going to Craigslist and searching for people to have affairs with. The Internet allows them to act out their fantasies and urges in secret, and it is all just one click away. It starts with curiosity—someone just wanting to take a look—then moves to them acting on it. She shared how she has clients who have reconnected with old boyfriends or girlfriends on Facebook. These would be people they would never have had access to in the past. Normally, they wouldn't have sought them out, called, or emailed them, but "friending" them on Facebook seems so harmless and easy. She tells her clients, "When you get married, all opposite-sex relationships you have had should be shared as a couple. This openness can protect you both from affairs more than anything else."

Dr. May offers the following signs that a couple should look out for to head off a Facebook affair:

SIGNS YOU ARE HEADED FOR A FACEBOOK AFFAIR

- You are lonely or emotionally disconnected in your marriage and you use Facebook or social media to distract you.
- While you are on Facebook, you intentionally look to see what someone of the opposite sex is posting and what they are doing, and feel the need to make comments that draw attention to yourself.
- You can't wait to read what these people post back to you and, during your day, think about the person and what you can post or comment about that they will read.
- You also start sending private messages to this person so others can't see what you are reading.
- If your spouse finds out about it and asks you to defriend or cut off contact, and you can't or don't want to.

Ten Questions to Discuss with Your Spouse about Facebook

1. How much time each day is an acceptable amount of time to spend on Facebook?
2. Are there times during the week that should be Facebook-free?
3. When accepting friend requests from others, who is OK to accept requests from and who is not?
4. Who are the types of people from your past that are OK to search for on Facebook and who are not?
5. How personal can updates and comments get with the sharing of details about yourself, your spouse, your family, your work, and your life?
6. Are there any words, terms, or phrases that will not be typed and shared publicly? What topics are off-limits to write about in updates and comments?
7. What types of Facebook friends are OK to have private communications with using the FB Message and Chat feature?
8. What should occur if a Facebook friend crosses the line?
9. How will you and your spouse connect offline about your Facebook experience?
10. Would we be happier in our marriage if neither of us engages Facebook?[18]

Repairing Marriage after a Facebook Affair

If you have had a Facebook affair, how can you repair your marriage after it? This is an important question, since this is becoming more and more common. Dr. May offers the following suggestions.

The first step is to be honest and confess the truth. Your spouse may be shocked and angry. Being defensive or minimizing the affair only breeds more distrust. As painful as it is, honesty, admitting what is going on in your life and marriage that made an affair an option, is the place to begin healing. Recognize that for you, it may have been harmless, but it is still painful to your spouse. Both of you need to go through the healing process, to become physically and emotionally available to each other. Seek professional help if you can't get through these steps together.

So how does a couple become a "safe haven" for each other? They need to spend time together. When you do this, you become familiar with each other. This familiarity brings comfort to both of you. We were raised in South Africa, and in Afrikaans there is a saying: *"Ek het jou lief."* Translated, it literally means, "I hold your heart." The idea of holding and protecting each other's hearts is a powerful image and is what love is all about. Let your spouse know they can trust you with their heart. Being a safe haven means you must become trustworthy, predictable, and dependable.

What We Can Do about It

The digital invasion has created an intimacy deficiency. And old-fashioned intimacy is at the hallmark of our relationships and is about sharing our emotions and feelings. This deeper level of connecting is what most of us talk about wanting in our relationships but struggle to attain it. Technology is a good place to share information but not a good avenue to convey our feelings and emotions. Don't confuse digital intimacy for true intimacy.

Work on revealing your feelings in your relationships. This emotional bond created by your exchange of feelings will carry you through the hard times and allow you to stay connected even in the midst of conflict. Many people describe "real life" encounters with another person as a bother and "not as exciting" as an endless stream of online encounters. But these online encounters create the illusion of intimacy when in fact we are still emotionally disconnected.

Identify four or five key relationships you want to invest in. Make time for them in your daily schedule and enter into real conversations. You have been created for intimate relationships. Intimacy is about seeing each other clearly and completely with as little distortion as possible. In your relationships, try to have conversations with people, not just connections. True intimacy requires you share your feelings, your thoughts, and your heart. Real-life encounters are worth the effort and will bring glory to God and help your relationships thrive and flourish.

Discussion Questions

1. Were you aware of the growing epidemic of narcissism among our youth? Discuss your experience with narcissistic people.
2. Can you relate to the statement "We expect more from technology and less from each other"? How could you turn this around?

3. Have you, or anyone close to you, tried online dating? Share the experience.

4. If you have experienced any signs of Facebook depression, make a list of these signs and share the list with someone else. What steps are you taking to deal with this depression?

5. If you use Facebook and other social media for business, what are the challenges you face? Discuss some practical solutions.

6. Which of the "Steps to Preventing Facebook Affairs" do you and/or your spouse need to take?

6

More Serious Cyber Problems

The greatest threat to the body of Christ, to the church, to families, and to the individual Christian is the pervasive, destructive pornography available through the Internet.

Josh McDowell

While we are focusing primarily on the more common challenges that parents, educators, and church leaders face from the Internet and cyber world, it would be remiss of us not to highlight the more serious challenges that our information superhighway is creating. In this chapter, we want to briefly cover some of these more serious disorders, which need further discussion. Unfortunately, these more severe problems do not lend themselves to "self-help" strategies, and the reader may need to seek professional help for the problems we discuss in this chapter.

It was Marshall McLuhan, borrowing a statement from Winston Churchill, prime minister of England during World War II, who said, "We become what we behold. We shape our tools and then our tools shape us." The same is true of our digital technology. We invented it, we shaped it, but now it is shaping and controlling us. But what is even more disquieting is the *way* technology now shapes us. We believe it is far more destructive than we originally thought it could be.

Destructive Consequences from Internet Pornography

Internet pornography is at the top of our list of concerns. Josh McDowell, a Christian apologist, writer, and author or co-author of some seventy-seven books, recently wrote a position paper on this topic entitled "Just1ClickAway." In it he states:

> An insidious intruder is putting your children at risk. It is systematically stalking your children, and sadly, most parents and Christian leaders are oblivious to it. We are in the midst of a social media revolution that is allowing a corrupt and perverted morality to have direct access to our children.[1]

We agree completely with Josh that Internet pornography is one of the most serious predicaments facing us in our digital world. Families are under attack. With just one click of a key on a smartphone, iPad, or laptop, you can access some of the most vile images and sexually graphic pornography imaginable. The Internet has drastically increased the ease of access to pornography, not just to adults, but to children and teens as well. Internet pornography is number one in all categories of Internet sales. It is accessed more frequently than games, travel, jokes, health, weather, and jobs combined.[2] The number one search term used on the web's engines is "sex."[3] The average age of the first exposure to Internet pornography is now eleven years, and some studies say it is as early as eight and a half years of age.[4] According to a study cited in the *Washington Post*, more than 11 million teenagers now view Internet porn on a regular basis.[5]

Regrettably, many Christians tend to avoid this topic. For some it is just denial, as if they don't want to face up to the fact that someone close to them might be accessing pornography. It is also an embarrassing topic, and so many families avoid discussing it. When a serious pornography addiction is discovered, many feel at a loss to know what they should do about it. We trust what we offer will help in preventing and overcoming pornography addiction. We believe that our silence as Christians on many sexual issues needs to be broken so parents can face the reality of what might be going on in their digital world. Silence on sexual matters can do more harm than good.

Our world is changing rapidly. It was not too long ago that the worst a boy could do was to sneak a peek at a *Playboy* magazine he found tucked away in the back of a drawer. Or, according to the stories I (Dr. Hart) have heard many men tell, their fathers deliberately left these magazines lying around, believing that it was a "rite of passage" for their sons and a way to learn about sex. High-gloss, colorful, and titillating, these nude magazines lined the racks in every supermarket and magazine store, inviting boys to steal a look just when their sex hormones were maturing. But many parents didn't realize what power these sexual images could have on a young boy's developing brain, even though they only depicted nudity.

What is more alarming is that experts are now telling us that our young men are, in effect, being neutered. In a CNN.com report, Dr. Philip Zimbardo, a world-renowned professor emeritus at Stanford University, and psychologist Nikita Duncan report that overuse of video games and the pervasiveness of online porn is causing the "demise of guys."[6] The excessive use of video games and online porn in pursuit of the next exciting thing is creating a generation of risk-averse guys who are unable (and unwilling) to navigate the complexities and risks inherent to real-life relationships, school, and employment. Stories about this degeneration are rampant. They report that in 2005, a South Korean man went into cardiac arrest after playing a cyber game called "StarCraft" for nearly fifty continuous hours. In 2009, MTV's *True Life* highlighted the story of a man named Adam whose wife kicked him out of their home because "he couldn't stop watching porn." They further report that "young men—who use porn the most—are being digitally rewired in a totally new way that demands constant stimulation. And those delicate, developing brains are being catered to by video games and porn-on-demand, with a click of the mouse, in endless variety."[7]

The exposure of youth to inappropriate nudity and explicit sex takes place at a vulnerable stage of life. And this is why pornography has the power to create an obsession and addiction. Men, of course, have been the majority to suffer here, but many women are succumbing as well. Internet pornographers now target female audiences as well by drawing them into chat rooms. Their goal is to have women form relational bonds in these chat rooms, as women tend to focus more on relationships, whereas men focus more on body parts.

The Internet has also opened up a market for sexually explicit media that trumps everything we could have imagined. Pornography is no longer available just on street corners or back alleys, but it is available in every living room and bedroom. It is in every pocket that has a smartphone. While some men might hate and avoid it, many love and embrace it. Back in 1996, the Department of Justice issued the following warning: "Never before in the history of telecommunications media in the United States, has so much indecent (and obscene) material been so easily accessible by so many minors in so many American homes with so few restrictions."[8] It appears that we have not heeded this warning.

What many pornography addicts do not realize is that a lot of it is unreal. Back in the '70s, I (Dr. Hart) had a patient who was suffering from depression. He shared with me something of his life growing up in Hollywood, the son of a pornographic magazine publisher. His father allowed him to roam freely around the porn factory while photos were being taken and processed, and he shared a lot of the "inner" secrets of the business. What I found most illuminating was that the porn photos found in a typical magazine were never real. They were modified, adjusted, improved—blemishes removed, noses resized, and bodies enhanced—all to make the photos present perfection in every respect. Every picture is a fantasy, not reality. This explains why it is so difficult for those who become hooked on porn to adjust to real life and real intimate relationships. Who can compete with such perfection? When men grow up only seeing videos of sexual fantasies and images of women who do not represent real life, it is very difficult for them to accept reality. "Exaggerated beauty" is one of the destructive aspects of pornography and is one big lie that creates a fantasy life with perfect bodies that don't exist. Consequently, when young people grow up being exposed to these fantasies, they have great difficulty accepting what is real.

In his book *The Drug of the New Millennium—The Brain Science Behind Internet Pornography*, Mark Kastleman, author, researcher, and trainer in the mind-body science field, has done extensive research in the field of pornography and sexual addiction prevention and recovery.[9] He claims that there is an epidemic of this addiction sweeping across America and much of the world. Parents and spouses are desperate for answers. Clergy and counselors are inundated and searching for solutions. It is estimated that over 60 million people in the United States are addicted to Internet pornography at some level and that nine out of ten children between age eight and sixteen have been exposed. Every variety of Internet pornography is instantly available to anyone, regardless of age or gender. No one is immune! The most devastating super drug in history is attacking our children and teenagers!

Kastleman presents a masterful analysis of how pornography destroys the mental and spiritual capacity of its victims, and we recommend this outstanding book to all parents, educators, and religious leaders.

The diagram below illustrates his model. He calls it the "Internet Pornography Funnel." At the top of the funnel, the individual is in reality or real time. The moment he or she starts looking at pornography, the brain narrows its focus under the influence of an "eroto-toxin." A response is triggered that is so powerful that we have no natural built-in mechanism to cope with it. Internet pornography draws you from reality into a fantasy world where fantasy reigns supreme. In this "Fantasy Addict Time," you give up your ability to think clearly and lose touch with real time.[10]

Figure 2

Internet Pornography Funnel Effect

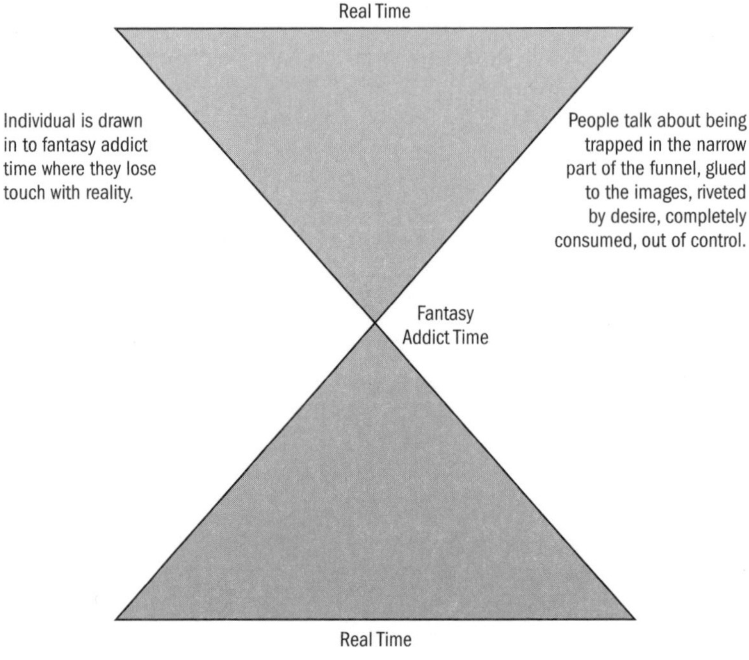

Real Time

Individual is drawn in to fantasy addict time where they lose touch with reality.

People talk about being trapped in the narrow part of the funnel, glued to the images, riveted by desire, completely consumed, out of control.

Fantasy Addict Time

Real Time

In my (Dr. Hart's) book *The Sexual Man*, I describe how a group of students at Duke University got together to share their experience of growing up with pornography. Discussing it as a group, they began to realize just how distorted sex had become to them. Nearly all were having great difficulty in forming close relationships with real women.[11] It's an eye-opening story worth reading. If that is what constituted pornography in the '80s, modern porn on the Internet is a million times further from real life. Pornography, in the form of "virtual sex," is becoming our next major menace. By the term "virtual sex," we mean a pornographic experience that is so realistic that you feel you are a part of what is going on. A whole new industry is inventing gadgets and computer programs that will take the sexual experience to a whole new level of stimulation and simulation. While rudimentary sexual toys have been around as long as porn magazines and videos, future Internet sex experiences will have "hands free" stimulation gadgets that can mimic the vibrations and sensations of sexual parts of the body, supposedly providing an experience so real that you can hardly tell the difference between it and reality.[12] Coupled with 3D virtual videos with contact lenses you can wear that superimpose an image of someone else, these sophisticated devices will take sexual experiences to a whole new level. Already, plans are afoot in some cities to create "pay-per-view" hotel rooms that provide this enhanced, virtual porn experience. This will increase the difficulty of being satisfied with a real-life sexual relationship.

Breaking Free

Alarming as these future developments are, at least to us, for the remainder of this section our focus will be on current pornography practices, and how it should be prevented and treated. As in many aspects of our digital world, there are those who would argue that Internet pornography is not addicting, nor is it a threat to marital relationships. They cite couples that used pornography to enhance their sexual arousal or overcome sexual inhibitions. Although this may be true for a few couples, we need to accept that the risk of this practice becoming addicting is high for one or both of them. Then, how does one return to "normal" sexual practices as a couple when you have become dependent on porn?

We also want to raise awareness that there is a link between Internet pornography and sex trafficking. The key ingredient is the belief that women are sexual commodities, and Internet pornography is the vehicle used to teach and train this belief. If you or someone you know is watching Internet pornography, they in turn are supporting this belief and fueling the sex trafficking industry. My (Dr. Frejd's) daughter spent a month this summer as a missionary in India with Rahab's Rope,[13] an organization that is working to prevent and stop sexual and human trafficking.

In the two studies of Christian sexuality previously mentioned that I (Dr. Hart) and my daughter Dr. Catherine Hart Weber conducted several years ago, we explicitly explored the issue of whether the use of pornography enhanced marital sex. These studies covered over 500 men and 2,000 women. In our male research, we found absolutely no benefit to marital sex that could be attributed to pornography. Over 30 percent of the men we studied reported that their early exposure to pornography had been destructive to their current sexuality.[14] Eighty percent of the men admitted that pornography was definitely degrading to ordinary women. In our female study, 21 percent of women reported being exposed to pornography as a child.[15] Their main concern was how the use of pornography in any situation was upsetting. Instead of enhancing their sexual experience, it inhibited it. Pornography was always seen to be degrading to women.

What are some of the destructive consequences that we see when pornography reaches the level of addiction?

DESTRUCTIVE CONSEQUENCES FROM PORNOGRAPHY

- There is a decreased desire for sexual intimacy with the user's spouse.
- The user develops a preoccupation with pornography to the extent that it intrudes into their work and may lead to dismissal. It can lead to whole days being lost to online porn use or self-stimulation and fantasy.
- The long hours of preoccupation with porn can also lead to emotional disorders such as irritability and depression.
- Pornography addiction can lead to an escalation of the problem with increasing amounts of time being spent masturbating or viewing progressively more arousing, intense, or bizarre sexual

content. (Just as in other addictions, there is an increased desire for satisfaction.)

- Porn addiction can lead to living a secret or double sexual life that is known fully only to the addict.

- The addict is unable to stop the use of pornography despite severe consequences or previous attempts to do so, or mounting pressure from loved ones.

Cybersex and Cyber-Affairs

Also known as computer sex, Internet sex, netsex, mudsex, and Tiny-Sex, cybersex is a "virtual" sex encounter over the Internet, usually with a total stranger. It involves two or more persons sending each other explicit messages or pictures detailing their sexual experience. It is a form of sexual role-play in which the participants pretend they are having a fantastic sexual experience. Cybersex is designed to stimulate sexual feelings and fantasies. In one form of cybersex, participants describe their actions and responses to their chat partner in mostly written form, such as emails or texting, so as not to provide any sort of voice recognition.

Cybersex can include masturbation, and in some cases can result in a real-life sexual encounter with other persons. Cybersex can then become a cyber-affair. It is generally believed that imagination and suspension of one's real-life beliefs are critically important in these behaviors. In other words, it fosters a "fantasy sexual experience," not a real one.

Given the high degree of sexual distortion in our world today, it is not surprising there are those who tout the benefits of cybersex. They claim that it can cure sexual disorders and liberate the sexually repressed, as well as provide some novel sexual experience for couples who are separated by work assignments or travel. But suggesting that cybersex between total strangers is appropriate to satisfy what are often distorted and unsavory expressions of sexual desire are not something we condone. Yes, cybersex may reduce the risk of exposure to a sexually transmitted disease, or prevent pregnancy, but it fosters a form of sexual promiscuity that goes beyond what should be considered normal.

There is nothing commendable about cybersex. When done with strangers or secretly behind a spouse's back, it is a form of betrayal.

It is also perilous, as cybersex participants often log their interaction without the other's knowledge. If disclosed at a later stage to others or the public, it can destroy a person's reputation.

That cybersex can be destructive to marriages or a close relationship is quite obvious. One doesn't need expensive or sophisticated research to come to this conclusion. The activity itself creates a special type of enhanced sexual experience that can surpass regular marital sex, by the very fact that you are doing something that runs contrary to one's values. The guilt produced in such acts, as in many sexual addictions, increases the adrenaline component of sexual arousal. When adrenaline stimulation becomes paired with sexual arousal, it gives an above-normal sexual experience. We see this form of sexual enhancement in rape, sexual crimes, and serial killings. This is the reason many men cheat on their wives. You may feel guilty afterward, but this "low" feeling only sets you up for the next "high"—a classic addictive process.[16]

Sexting

It is not surprising that texting, having become such an integral part of our lives, has also seen a rise in how it is used sexually. According to the Pew Research Center's Internet and American Life Project, 4 percent of cell-phone-using teenagers aged twelve to seventeen say they have sent sexually suggestive nude or nearly nude images or videos of themselves to someone else via text messaging. Fifteen percent say they have received such images of someone they know via a text message.[17] "Teens explained to us how sexually suggestive images have become a form of relationship currency," says Amanda Lenhart, senior research specialist with the Pew Research Center. Her report goes on to reveal that teens who are more intense cell phone users are more likely to receive sexually suggestive images. One high school girl we talked with told us, "Yes, I have received and sent these types of pictures often. Boys usually ask for them. One boy I really liked asked for them. And I felt like if I didn't do it, he wouldn't continue to talk to me. At the time, it was no big deal, but now looking back it was definitely inappropriate and over the line." The revealing pictures of herself, in the possession of someone she no longer wanted to date, continues to haunt her.

We know that teenagers (and some adults) often have difficulty with impulse control. They can't delay gratification, and with the advancement of our cell phone abilities, it's easier than ever to use technology unwisely without considering the consequences. Yes, it is normal for teenagers to explore their sexuality, but sexting is not the way to do it.

One of the real dangers of sexting is the legal implications. Sending sexually explicit pictures of people under the age of eighteen is a felony in all fifty states, even if the sender is the subject. Receiving these images is also illegal. Sexting carries the possibility of being charged as a sex offender or child pornographer. I (Dr. Frejd) heard this week of a story about a sixteen-year-old boy who has already served a one-year sentence and is waiting a retrial for receiving a sext from a fifteen-year-old girl and resending it. When released from prison, he will be registered as a sex offender for the rest of his life.

It is imperative that parents take steps to protect their teenage children by educating them and intentionally informing them of these laws and dangers. They need to refrain from sexting no matter how much they think they can trust the recipient. Tell your child that, if they receive a sext, to delete it immediately and tell the sender to stop sending these texts.

The other danger of sexting is social. Most sex images sent to a friend get sent on to someone else, beyond the original recipient. So you can never tell where it will end up. They may forward it, post it on a public forum, or even post it on a computer at school.

If sexting becomes habitual, what can parents do to break the habit? As with all major sexually related addictions, self-help isn't enough. The sexting addict needs to seek professional help and face the fact there will be quite a battle ahead. Unlike substance abuse, where a major biological illness can often bring an addict to his or her senses, behavioral addictions like pornography are not always seen as life threatening, and as such, not given the serious attention that is needed to overcome it.

Fortunately, there are a growing number of organizations on the Internet that offer help. A search for your particular location should yield some resources. These are some websites that are worthy of exploration:

- http://www.sexualrecovery.com/pornography-addiction.php
- www.recoverynation.com/
- www.christiananswers.net/q-eden/sexaddictiontips.html
- www.xxxchurch.com

A website that offers healing for wives who've been hurt from adultery or porn addiction can be found at

- http://www.blazinggrace.org/index.php?page=healing-from-adultery-porn-for-wives

One Solution: A Healthy Theology of Sex

All of our serious sexually related cyber problems have one common trait: a deficient "theology of sex." Teaching your children a healthy theology of sex is one of the greatest gifts you can give them. Human sexuality and sex are good gifts from God. Yes, sex is good! Marriage, of course, is God's intended framework for us to express our sexuality. Sex consummates a marriage, and its major function is procreation, but it is also a way of expressing love to our spouse. Lastly, it is for enjoyment and pleasure. Sin degrades and distorts sexuality through lust and sensuality. This occurs when sex is linked with violence, abuse, and rape, and through Internet pornography. Sex in marriage is character forming because the partners must learn to delay gratification at times, and remain committed to confining sexual satisfaction to their spouse. The Theology of Sex Initiative offered by the National Association of Evangelicals expresses it well:

> God gave us a very good gift when He created us as sexual beings. Although our view of sexuality and our experiences of it are marred by sin and imperfectly expressed, our task is to bring the redemptive light of the gospel to sex. So we advocate and seek a sexuality that is joyful, nonexploitive, respectful and aligned with God's creative intent.[18]

The time is now to seize the opportunity and live out a biblically based theology of God's design for our sexuality.

Cyberstalking

While there is no universally accepted definition of *cyberstalking*, the term generally describes the use of the Internet, email, or other electronic communication devices to stalk another person. The stalking generally includes some form of harassment or threatening behavior. It is repeated over and over again, and in some instances has led to the victim taking his or her own life. There is usually some grudge or need for revenge behind the stalking behavior, or the stalker does it just for the pleasure it gives them.

While there are laws designed to protect children from online predators, especially sexual, a lot of stalking behavior is more annoying than criminal and falls short of being illegal behavior. This can be a problem for parents trying to protect their children, as they have no legal recourse. So, parents need to take this matter seriously and try to find a solution themselves.

The Internet invites this behavior because of its ease of access and the anonymity one can maintain. It can also reach across oceans to other countries. Cyberstalking often follows a previous connection between the two parties, but can be done anonymously by jealous friends or total strangers who have a vicious and punitive streak and take pleasure in hurting others. The perpetrator may be a very disturbed person, so do not try to confront the stalker on your own. Get whatever help and assistance you can from school or other authorities. Also, remember that a stalker can disguise his or her identity or even masquerade under someone else's identity.

In addition to reporting the stalking to the appropriate Internet server, get professional help for a family member who may be the victim of cyberstalking, then report any risky harassment to the appropriate legal authorities. If your child is being cyberstalked by someone in school, report it to the school authorities. Even if a threat is not seen to be serious by the perpetrator or the perpetrator's parents, it can have devastating effects on victims, as we have seen in young people committing suicide when they have been harassed. No one should have to suffer such cruel behavior.

All the evidence suggests that cyberstalking is a growing problem, so unfortunately we will be seeing a lot more of it to come in the future.

Cyberbullying

Closely linked to the problem of cyberstalking, is *cyberbullying*. Cyberbullying usually involves a child. It could be a preteen or teen that is harassed, humiliated, or embarrassed by another child. Cowards can now play at bullying because it can be done at a safe distance.

To experience cyberbullying can be very upsetting. It can leave a permanent mark on a child's inner life and undermine self-esteem and creates many fears. Often a child can be a victim one moment, then a bully himself or herself the next. Kids often change roles, going from victim to bully and back again.

Unlike physical bullying, where a stronger, more overpowering child usually tries to dominate or punish a weaker child, cyberbullying can be done by a weaker person, hiding behind the safety of a computer and the Internet. They can conceal their identity, so the victim has no idea who the bully is.

Unlike physical bullying, digital bullies can remain virtually anonymous by using temporary email accounts, pseudonyms in chat rooms, instant messaging programs, or text messaging to mask their identity. This frees a child from normative and social constraints.

Cyberbullying can be as simple as continuing to send annoying emails or text messages to someone who has rejected them. But it may also include threats, sexual comments, name calling, and expressions of hate. Sometimes a group gangs up on a victim by making them the subject of ridicule and posting false statements about them on the Internet. The goal is nearly always to humiliate the victim.

How common is cyberbullying? A 2006 survey by Harris Interactive reported that 43 percent of United States teens have experienced some form of cyberbullying in the past year.[19] That's nearly every second child. An excellent resource on this topic we recommend is a book entitled *Cybersafe*, published by the American Academy of Pediatrics and authored by Gwenn Schurgin O'Keefe, MD.[20]

Internet Gambling

It is alarming to see how many forms of gambling are now available on the Internet, and how easy it is to bet on almost anything online through your smartphone, including poker, sports betting, bingo, lotteries, and horse racing. Every conceivable form of gambling that existed is now available on the Internet.

Mobile gambling, using wireless computers and smartphones, has made it possible for gamblers to "do their thing" while walking in the park or riding the bus to work. Funds are easily transferred back and forth, and no taxes are charged, by and large. While most United States banks prohibit the use of their debit cards for Internet gambling, plenty of other fund transfer services are readily available.

In researching this topic, we were quite alarmed to discover how easy it was to find an online gambling site, and how many people who never used to gamble now gamble on a regular basis. Many may well be on their way to achieving addiction status!

Estimates of the number of people who are diagnosed with a gambling addiction are difficult to find. It appears to range anywhere from 2 to 5 percent of the population in the United States. This may seem like a low percentage, but in real numbers it means that many millions of people are affected by it in the United States alone. Although more men than women suffer from pathological gambling, women are rapidly developing this disorder and could easily outpace men in the near future. Men tend to develop this disorder during their early teenage years, while women tend to develop it later and at a much faster rate than men do.

We believe that online gambling addiction is destructive to families, and have seen its effects on families we have counseled. What causes this addiction? The brain's pleasure system and the hormone dopamine are obviously implicated, and as in the other addictions, our society condones it to some extent.

Gambling is not just a single problem but has an effect on the whole family. And it is not just the robbing of family finances that is devastating. Statistics indicate that families of compulsive gamblers, including online gamblers, are more likely to experience domestic violence and child abuse. Children of problem gamblers are at a significantly higher risk of suffering from depression, behavior problems, and substance abuse.[21] Unfortunately this disorder does not respond well to treatment, and as many as two-thirds of those who begin treatment for a gambling disorder discontinue their treatment prematurely. It makes no difference whether treatment includes medication, psychotherapy, or both. It is a difficult habit to give up.

Online gamblers are just as resistant to getting treatment as other gamblers. Unlike drug or alcohol addictions that can cause you to lose your employment, gambling addictions are not as overtly threatening and are easier to ignore. One can maintain a measure of respectability while gambling online because it is not public, whereas drug or alcohol addiction often has some public display. Although there is no standardized treatment for pathological gambling, many people find it helpful to participate in Gamblers Anonymous (GA). As with alcoholism, one needs very strong support to facilitate recovery. And recovery from any addiction is better when combined with psychotherapy by a trained professional. So, if anyone in your family is an addicted online gambler, make sure they see an experienced professional who is competent in treating gambling addiction.

Internet Video Gaming Addictions

Internet gaming addiction is somewhat similar to pathological gambling, but because many see it as a form of entertainment, it is not as offensive. The addiction may involve the Internet, but many video games are now readily available through gaming gadgets like Xbox and PlayStation, so they don't need any Internet connection. These video gaming technologies are now firmly embedded in the cultural identity of American teenagers. As we write this book, it is estimated that 95 to 97 percent of our youth are playing video games of one sort or another. Video game addiction, also known as video game overuse, is the extreme use of video games to the extent that it interferes with daily life. Gaming addiction is a form of impulse control disorder. People with this impulse control disorder can't resist the urge to engage in behaviors that harm themselves or others and are disposed toward developing other addictions such as alcohol, drugs, eating disorders, and compulsive gambling. The impulse to play these games is overwhelming. Teens are the most vulnerable to gaming addictions, and their need to play can be obsessive to the extent it is harmful to themselves or to others.

The symptoms are similar to other psychological addictions. Some play for many hours each day, disregard personal hygiene, and become so involved with their gaming interactions that they ignore their broader lives. Instances have been reported in which players isolate themselves for long periods from family and friends or any form of social contact. It disrupts their sleep patterns and they focus entirely on their game achievements rather than on other life events. As a result, the gamer develops a lack of creativity and can become very moody if they can't play. As mentioned earlier, there are cases where young people in South Korea's gaming halls have been found dead, slumped over their gaming keyboards.

What causes gaming addiction? Again, the pleasure and reward system of the brain plays a major role in delivering extreme euphoria while gaming. This also explains why it is so addicting. Gaming provides a make-believe world for the gamer, providing an escape from the real world. In the case of a gamer in China who committed suicide, the head of one software association was quoted as saying: "In the hypothetical world created by such games, they become confident and gain satisfaction, which they cannot get in the real world."[22] Motivational psychologists also believe that many video games satisfy basic psychological needs, and players often continue to play because of rewards and the connection it provides to other players.[23] In fact, CNN has just reported that "gaming is now a 'need to have' category, not a 'nice to have' category for mobile devices."[24] More than 60 percent of users now regularly play games on their mobile devices.

Gaming Risk Addiction

Parents need to realize that manufacturers of these video games deliberately design them to be highly stimulating and to give an adrenaline rush. Some video games take forty hours to play through. Other games, like the massively multiplayer online role-playing games, called "MMORPGs," are interactive and are based on scenarios that are unpredictable. These types of games pose the greatest challenge because they are the most addicting. This has led to a new phenomenon in young men called "failure to launch," and gaming addictions are a large contributor. A Life Coaching organization called Forte Strong that has a "Failure To Launch Program" says, "Young men have been raised by video games and the Internet. Sometimes it becomes an addiction and sometimes it just prevents these guys from going out into the real world to socialize, get jobs, and learn valuable life skills that lead to independence."[25]

Communicating with your child is the key to educating him or her in developing healthier play habits. Inform your child about the addictive nature of these games and help them to set limits with their playing time.

Gaming has become a serious problem for countries like South Korea and China. South Korea has had to open video gaming addiction treatment centers[26] to deal with their crisis. This may well be the next step we have to take in the United States. For parents who need help in dealing with children who are extreme gamers, we recommend "On-line Gamers Anonymous." It uses a traditional twelve-step, self-help, support and recovery program for gamers who are suffering from the adverse effects of excessive gaming. This organization also provides a variety of message boards, daily online chat meetings, a Saturday and Wednesday Skype meeting, and other tools for recovery, healing, and support.

GamingAddiction.net was formed in 2011 to promote responsible gaming for Internet games, online gambling, and fantasy sports.[27] They offer surveys for gamers and the people that care about them. They advocate a simple three-pronged approach to responsible gaming:

1. Understand what gaming is.
2. Solve problems that are created by excessive gaming.
3. Act out the solution and live a healthier life free of gaming addiction.

Addiction Risk for Video Games

Kevin Roberts, a nationally recognized expert on video gaming addiction and the author of *Cyber Junkie: Escaping the Gaming and Internet Trap*, out of his experience in running support groups to help cyber addicts who struggle to get their lives back on track, offers the following risk ratings for major games. The risk goes from 1 to 10, 10 being the severest.[28]

- *Puzzle Games*:
  Tetris, Solitaire, FreeCell—Addiction Risk 2
- *Physical Simulation*:
  Dance Dance Revolution and Guitar Hero—Addiction Risk 2
- *Old School Games*:
  Nintendo 64, PlayStation 1, Sega's Dreamcast—Addiction Risk 3
- *Educational Games*:
  TheorySpark, Gettysburg!, Total War—Addiction Risk 4
- *Manage and Control Game*:
  Black & White, RollerCoaster Tycoon—Addiction Risk 5
- *First Person Shooter Games*:
  Counter-Strike, Halo, and Call of Duty—Addiction Risk 7
- *Real Time Strategy Games*:
  Command & Conquer, Age of Empires, Empire Earth—Addiction Risk 7
- *The Narcotics of the Game World*—MMORPGs (Massively Multiple Online Role-Playing):
  RuneScape—Addiction Risk 7,
  World of Warcraft—Addiction Risk 10

Virtual Worlds

In her book *Alone Together*, Sherry Turkle, professor of social studies at MIT, makes a strong case for how technology presents itself as the "architect of our intimacies."[29] In a sense, the digital world substitutes itself for reality and allows places to create "virtual worlds" where they can build an avatar (a computer-generated false ego) or substitute an imaginary social life. The Internet can even raise a "virtual baby" that can wake you, demand feeding, and cry just like a real baby. A recent report tells how a couple in South Korea, who had signed on to this virtual baby program, was spending most of their time attending to the virtual baby, while their real baby was left alone in a back room and eventually died of neglect.

Dr. Turkle explains that there are scores of people searching for a place where they can love their body, love their friends, and love their lives. The only problem is that when they find it on the Internet, it is all "virtual," not real. An example of this extreme form of escape from reality can be seen in a movement called Second Life, an online virtual world launched in June 2003.[30] A number of free "viewers" enable Second Life users (called "residents") to interact with each other through "avatars" (the graphical representation of themselves in a character of their own design). Residents then explore the world (known as the "grid") and meet with other residents, to socialize or participate in group activities. All of this is supposed to make you achieve the ideal sort of person you long to be. For example, people can make themselves smarter, richer, more attractive, taller/shorter, younger, thinner, and more loved. Second Life is intended for people aged sixteen and over, and as of 2011 had about one million active users. Some may be able to do it as a game for a while and then go back and face reality. The problem is, many don't return to reality and the consequences can be devastating.

We need to look beyond how we now use our computers and explore how the digital world will affect our lives in the future. With all due respect to "Second Lifers," you still have to raise your children, go to work, and earn a living in the real world. What we need is a digital world that can help us engage in reality and thrive, and not merely seek entertainment. Our "first life," lived to the fullest, is still the best life!

What Does the Future Hold?

While we have focused on just a few of the more serious cyber problems we now face, it is quite certain, judging by how fast these problems have developed, that we will be experiencing even more in the future.

While today's Internet is rapidly expanding with faster connections and growing Internet users, it is not surprising that we are quickly beginning to run out of "wireless space."

What does this all mean on a personal level? Well, it all depends on the extent to which we, as parents, teachers, social and political leaders, respond to and manage the future of our digital world. But where are we headed? As we close this chapter, we want to highlight some of the trends we see and invite you to reflect on them as you prepare yourself and your family to be vigilant and wise in using the digital world:

Trend #1: Government agencies are becoming increasingly concerned about our safety, at the national and personal level. We need to be more careful when sending personal and financial information over the Internet. Security and privacy are the most immediate short-term challenges facing us today. With the decentralizing of the global network, nothing is private anymore if we don't take steps to protect our information.

Trend# 2: The growth of the web has encouraged online consumer purchasing. In the years ahead, more and more people will rely on e-commerce. We anticipate that the day may come when stores, as we know them, will be irrelevant. Most shopping could be done online with delivery direct to your home. While this sounds like a good thing, it will require even more vigilance in protecting personal identity and preventing identity theft.

Trend # 3: Digital technology will expand into our cars and other forms of transport. Already Ford has announced a slew of gadgets that are available to the driver, including Ford SYNC's capability to turn a phone's data connection into a Wi-Fi hotspot. With Mobile-Ease, the vehicle's audio system will automatically mute when a call is placed or received, and advanced voice-recognition technology will enable drivers and passengers to dial using simple voice commands. Government agencies are already raising concerns about these additional distractions to driving. We are having enough trouble bringing texting while driving under control; it seems many other battles over Internet induced distractions lie ahead.

Trend # 4: In the years ahead, according to Bill Gates, people will increasingly rely on computers and other digital gadgets to communicate and be entertained.[31] For this to be a safe digital engagement, we have to make the Internet as secure as we can. It is a long-term challenge and we are bound to make a lot of mistakes on the way. Some Internet security and privacy experts believe that privacy now DOES NOT EXIST. According to Steve Rambam, private investigator specializing in Internet privacy, "Privacy is dead—so get over it."[32] For us to ignore this lack of Internet privacy will have serious consequences in the future.

What We Can Do about It

We started out this chapter stating that Internet pornography is the greatest threat of our digital invasion. We believe the time is coming where your smartphone, iPad, and such will come with a warning label stating, "Excessive use of this digital device could be hazardous to your health."

This invasion is impacting our marriages and families in devastating ways, and we are encouraging you to take a proactive approach. The vast majority of adult pornography addicts were first exposed and hooked as teenagers. An Internet accountability tool like Covenant Eyes installed on all your family's digital devices could offer much needed protection. Covenant Eyes monitors the sites visited and sends a report to an accountability partner you select.

My (Dr. Frejd's) family has installed this accountability tool and are aware of the value it offers. This online transparency is the best defense against this dangerous invasion to you and your family. As the parent, you should be the one to teach your children about sex, love, and relationships. The most important impact on your child's sex and attitude and behavior is yours.

Discussion Questions

1. Discuss Josh McDowell's opening statement to this chapter that "the greatest threat to the body of Christ, to the church, to families, and to the individual Christian is the pervasive, destructive pornography available through the Internet." Do you agree or disagree with his statement?
2. Have you experienced any "sexting" in your family or the family of a friend? How was it handled and what was the outcome?

3. What has been your family's or friends' experience with cyberbullying?

4. Has any form of video gaming impacted your family or close friends? What was the game, and what about it did you find troubling?

5. Do you agree that online gambling can be as destructive to a family as regular gambling? Why?

6. Which of the future trends in the digital world we identify at the close of this chapter are you most concerned about? Why?

7

Overcoming Digital Addictions

I had a life once . . . now I have a computer.

Author unknown

Spending an evening on the World Wide Web is much like
sitting down to a dinner of Cheetos . . . two hours later
your fingers are yellow and you're no longer hungry, but
you haven't been nourished.

Clifford Stoll

As we begin writing this chapter, an alarming report has just been
published on CNN.com. entitled "Is the Internet Hurting Children?"
It states the following:

The explosive growth of social media, smartphones and digital devices
is transforming our kids' lives, in school and at home. Research tells
us that even the youngest of our children are migrating online, using
tablets and smartphones, downloading apps. Consumer Reports reported last year that more than 7.5 million American kids under the
age of 13 have joined Facebook, which technically requires users to be
13 years old to open an account. No one has any idea of what all of
this media and technology use will mean for our kids as they grow up.[1]

The report goes on to say that by the time our children are two years old, more than 90 percent of them will have an "online history." At age five, more than 50 percent of them regularly interact with a computer or tablet device, and by seven or eight years of age, most children regularly play video games. It is no wonder, therefore, that we need to be extremely concerned about how addicting the cyber world is becoming for our children and teenagers. Teenagers now send an average of 3,300 text messages a month. Furthermore, by the time our children reach middle school, they spend more time with media than with their parents or teachers.

The Digital Addiction Heist

Internet addiction is probably the most common and fastest-growing addiction of our modern time. Internet use, overuse, and abuse have been among the most concentrated areas of psychological investigation for the past ten years. Everyone is at risk for becoming hooked to his or her digital device and being pulled into overuse of the cyber world to the extent that it can become an addiction. Addiction to some form of Internet use by our youth is illusive, little understood, and widely ignored, and its long-term effects largely disregarded. Millions of people send billions of messages and posts every day, so it is becoming increasingly difficult to detect where the boundary is between normal communication and obsessive and addicting communication.

To be objective in our examination of digital addictions, let us begin with this question: Is there really such a thing as an Internet or digital addiction? Should we not reserve the label "addiction" for alcohol, cocaine, or some other type of substance abuse?

There are many other technological diversions, besides the Internet and our digital world, that have in times past been labeled as addicting. The most obvious example is television. When first introduced, many expressed concern that it could become addicting. The critics of Internet addiction now argue that since we have adapted to widespread use of television, the Internet will soon settle down and in time become another innocuous form of amusement.

The most outspoken critics of the "Internet addiction" theory are those who thrive on the Internet. They flourish in their email, texting, smartphone, Facebook, and gaming, and don't want to be labeled as "addicts." In a sense they are right. There is a lot of digital engagement on the part of our youth that doesn't qualify as a form of addiction, even if this activity is excessive. We need to be careful in how widely we throw the "Internet addiction net." So, the next most obvious question that arises is, Just how much Internet engagement does it take to turn you into an addict? Where is the boundary between excessive and normal Internet activity?

Clarifying Addiction

Before proceeding, we need to clarify the true meaning of the term *addiction*. Back in 1990, I (Dr. Hart) wrote a book entitled *Healing Life's Hidden Addictions*.[2] I wrote it at a time when there was a major controversy brewing in the addiction arena as to whether behavior can be addicting. Many addictionologists were insisting that only drugs and alcohol can be addicting—not behaviors. On the other side, behavioral scientists were claiming that behaviors could be addicting. They went a bit too far with it and claimed that everyone was addicted to something. They cite such examples as shopaholics, golfaholics, jogging addicts, and parents addicted to their own children. Even falling in love with someone was considered by some to be an addiction. The need to see a potential addiction in almost any behavior had become unreasonable, and to many it sounded trivial, ridiculous, and even demeaning to those who suffered from "real" addictions. My book was an attempt to reconcile these opposing opinions and clarify what a true addiction really is.

We see addiction as a complex interaction of psychological, biological, neurological, and spiritual factors. In other words, it is not caused just by a behavior or a chemical but by a combination of both. Alcoholics will tell you that they are as much addicted to the smoke-filled pub, social gathering, and atmosphere as to the liquor itself. Some substances, like cocaine, can easily lead to an addiction, but many behaviors can as well. When a behavior is addicting, it is called a "process addiction," because it involves a "process" rather than a substance.

The perfect example of a process addiction is gambling. As I tried to show in my book, while a behavior doesn't need the ingestion of a substance to make it addicting, the behavior itself will release a chemical inside the brain that can facilitate or strengthen the addiction. An example I often cite here is that of "adrenaline addiction." Certain high-stimulation or risky behaviors, like bungee cord jumping, can trigger an adrenaline rush, an experience that feels exciting and pleasurable. If repeated, this could become an addiction to both the behavior and the thrill hormone, adrenaline. Thrill seekers know this phenomenon well, because the adrenaline surge is highly pleasurable and turns on our pleasure system. When overstimulated, the brain's dopamine system, the hormone messenger that triggers the brain's "pleasure system," can cause an addiction to the behavior that triggers it.[3]

We know that the brain hormone "endorphin" is released in long-distance running. It gives a runner a "high" because the endorphin's function is to block pain. The endorphin rush is the main underpinning of "jogger's addiction."

In summary, there is no doubt in our minds that the behaviors involved in many digital activities can lead to addictive behavior.

The Reality of Digital Addictions

The front cover of the July 2012 *Newsweek* read, "iCrazy: Panic. Depression. Psychosis. How Connection Addiction Is Rewiring Our Brains."[4] The article goes on to say that the brains of Internet addicts scan a lot like the brains of drug and alcohol addicts. Our digital gadgets acts like electronic cocaine to the brain.

This addiction is not a recent phenomenon. Back in 1995, early in the development of the computer and the expansion of the Internet, concern was already being expressed that it could be addicting. A prominent expert in this field, Dr. Kimberly Young founded the Center for Internet Addiction Recovery to promote research in this and related issues. In 1996, I (Dr. Hart) attended the American Psychological Association's annual conference where the first paper on such a topic was presented. It was entitled "Internet Addiction: The Emergence of a New Disorder." Dr. Young's study found that "marriages, dating relationships, parent-child relationships, and close friendships were disrupted by excessive use of the Internet. Dependents gradually spent less time with real people in their lives in exchange for solitary time in front of a computer."[5]

Internet Addiction Disorder, known as IAD, will be included in the 2013 *Diagnostic and Statistical Manual of Mental Disorder* (DSM-V), which is considered the bible of psychology, as a "real" disorder. The reality is that IAD is considered a grave national health crisis. A person is vulnerable to addiction when that person feels a lack of satisfaction in life, an absence of intimacy or strong connections to other people, a lack of self-confidence or compelling interests, or a loss of hope. Individuals who feel overwhelmed or who experience personal problems or who experience life-changing events, such as a recent divorce, relocation, or a death, can absorb themselves in a virtual world full of fantasy and intrigue. The Internet can become a psychological escape that distracts a user from a real-life problem or difficult situation. Internet users who suffer from multiple addictions are at the greatest risk to suffer from Internet addiction.

Who is at risk for developing such an addiction? It is mostly the digital natives because they are more heavily involved in using digital technology and are being thrust into an educational system that uses digital technology extensively. But presently the gap between an "Internet addict" and the average person is thin to nonexistent. According to *Parenting* magazine, moms are the new Internet junkies![6] Many young mothers are addicted to blogs, message boards, and virtual-world sites like Second Life. In the most extreme cases, addicts don't bathe, they neglect their children, and they use drugs to help them stay up later for more Internet time. So why is the Internet so appealing to new moms? One of the reasons is that moms are alone for most of the day, and they're desperate for someone to talk to and find it in an online community. Moms turn to the online world to feel like they're not alone, and it becomes an escape to turn to whenever they feel stressed. It can also become a way to express themselves. In Second Life, a free 3-D virtual world where users can socialize, connect, and create using free voice and text chat, moms can create online images of themselves and can become anyone they desire to be. As a clinical psychologist, I (Dr. Hart) seriously question whether this is a healthy activity. It may be entertaining, but most users use it for more than entertainment. They are literally trying to live a "second life."

Components and Consequences

Internet addictions share the following four components:

1. *Excessive use*, often associated with a loss of sense of time or a neglect of basic drives and duties.
2. *Withdrawal symptoms*, including feelings of anger, tension, and/or depression when the computer is inaccessible.

3. *Tolerance*, including the need for upgraded computer equipment, more software programs, and longer hours of use. (In the addiction world, *tolerance* refers to how the body can get used to a medication so that you no longer get the same effect. In addictions it means you have to take more and more of a drug to get the same effect. The same is true for digital addictions—you need more and more.)

4. *Negative repercussions*, including arguments, family abuse, lying, poor achievement, social isolation, and fatigue.

And what are the consequences facing those who are Internet addicted? Pretty much the same as in other addictions:

- The important relationships that need nurturing will increasingly be neglected. This could result in more marriage failures, affairs (the Internet makes it easy to find needy partners), and family breakdowns (either parent neglecting their children or children avoiding their parents).

- Loss of employment, because of excessive use of the Internet for personal uses while at work. Or, the distraction of the Internet interfering with work effectiveness.

- Loss of sleep. Where excessive use of the Internet at home and late at night can lead to insomnia or just plain "sleep robbing." Lack of sleep is now linked to obesity, Type 2 diabetes, and the development of heart disease.

- Diminished energy, not just from sleep deprivation, but also from excessive digital engagement in general.

- Health problems associated with sitting for long periods, including eyestrain, carpal tunnel syndrome, headaches, backaches, and obesity.

- Internet addiction opens the pleasure-center door on a lot of other addictions, such as gambling, gaming, and pornography, as well as drugs and alcohol.

What Do ALL Addictions Have in Common?

The Internet and its applications have grown enormously, so it's not surprising that the term *Internet addiction* covers a broad range of activities. We have examined some aspects of these in more detail in other chapters, but now we will focus on the Internet in general.

How common is Internet addiction? A national study conducted by a team from Stanford University's School of Medicine estimates that nearly one in eight Americans suffer from at least one sign of problematic Internet use; many think it is higher than this.[7] All addictions have a common base and consequence, and in the long run, they all undermine healthy living.

They can also destroy family relationships and impact the lives of children. One mom we interviewed shared with us how her Internet addiction had impacted her family. Her use of Facebook had become excessive. It didn't happen suddenly but crept up slowly. Week by week her use of Facebook increased while her two small girls played in another room. At first she would feel guilty about the long time she spent on the Internet, neglecting her children, and each time she went back to her computer she reassured herself that she was only going to do a quick check on her Facebook. But before she realized it, an hour or more had passed. Her children started to complain that she never played with them. "Not now, Honey, Mommy's busy" was her typical response.

Then one day, after one of her children had fallen and hurt herself, she had a sudden wake-up call. "What if while I was Facebooking one of my children had a serious accident?" She realized that she was neglecting her kids while wasting precious time playing on the Internet. "More than this," she said, "I was missing out on the precious time I could be spending with them. I had become a slave to social media. I interacted with plenty of people on any given day, but I neglected my own two daughters." She immediately took steps to limit her Facebook and Internet time.

When mothers spend hours on the Internet, their addiction is bound to take a toll on their neglected children. Some liken social media to the old-fashioned "back fence" chats that homebound mothers engaged in. But this is no comparison. Back-fence chat time was limited by circumstance. But nowadays, mothers "multitask" and tweet or Facebook, often neglecting essential chores. And this is not healthy for mothers or their children.

Internet addictions share many of the characteristics of other addictions. These are the main features of all addictions:

- Addictions remove us from our true feelings, providing a form of escape from the unpleasant aspects of life. In many cases, one uses the Internet excessively in order to cope with social situations that are out of control. For instance, a husband who is unhappy with his marriage could swamp his life with Internet activities. Similarly, someone who is not performing well at work could find an escape in the digital world.

- Addictive behavior takes control of the addict to the extent that it exceeds all logic or reason. The true addict has feelings but may not acknowledge them.

- Addictions take the pleasure system of the brain captive. Only the addiction provides pleasure, but robs the center of other pleasures.

- The addiction takes priority over all other life issues. All addicts develop an obsession over their addictive behavior and think only of the moment they can get back to their addiction.

- Addicts always deny that their addiction is out of control and cannot see anything bad in their behavior.

- All addictions are, in a sense, also substance addictions, when you consider that the body becomes "hooked" on the underlying biochemical changes.

How Does an Internet Addiction Form?

Understanding the underlying mechanisms of addiction can help prevent this expanding problem. The similarities are both psychological and physical. For example, individuals addicted to alcohol or other drugs develop a social relationship with their drug. It is a relationship that takes precedence over all other relationships, including spouses and children. Digital addicts need their "high" merely to feel normal. They substitute unhealthy relationships for healthy ones. They opt for temporary pleasure rather than for deeper, more intimate relationships.

Can Internet addiction lead to other types of addiction, or can other addictions lead to Internet addictions? The same transfer can take place from one Internet addiction to another addiction. It is called a "generalization of addiction." For instance, if someone has an addiction to card gambling, he or she will almost certainly be prone to Internet gambling. Another example is someone addicted to shopping can transfer their addiction from the local mall to online stores. It is well known that an addiction to one risky and exciting behavior can set you up to become addicted to other risk-taking behaviors.

Where the Internet really outdoes other addictions is in its easy access to many addicting behaviors. A bungee cord addict may have to drive a long distance in order to perform the jump, but the Internet is everywhere, providing quick and easy access to the addiction. Christian believers need to be educated on how to deal with the temptations that come with this easy access to the Internet.

Why Is Texting So Prone to Addiction?

The rise in real-time text-based communications—such as Facebook, Twitter, instant messaging—has brought about compacted, new language communication tools. While they seem innocent on the surface, they have the potential to be very addicting.

Texting would seem to be the least likely to become addicting. After all, it does not usually contain any message of substance. But it is now one of the most common activities used in our culture. Sophisticated smartphones are tailored for texting and instant messaging, and digital natives are experts at it.

As a digital immigrant, you may never have received a text message from a texter. Therefore, it is likely you have no idea what a message like this means: "ABITHIWTITB!" Let us help you. It translates "A bird in the hand is worth two in the bush." Mostly, texting uses just a single letter of a word, or an abbreviation, to replace whole words or sentences. It has enormous advantages. It is very quick to type and send. Teenagers' thumbs can fly across tiny keyboards and send a message in the wink of an eye. Of course, there is not much depth in the content, but texting is not about content! Many text messages look like they have been written in a foreign language.

Researchers have taken a close look at why texting can become so addicting. They attribute it to a special form of "operant conditioning." This means that texting behavior is shaped, or reinforced, by its consequences. If you receive a constant flow of pleasurable messages, one after the other, you would probably become bored and stop looking for them, since they are pretty much all the same in content. If most of your text messages are mainly mundane, but then you get one that is very exciting or interesting, this "once only" exciting message reinforces you to keep looking for the next exciting message, no matter how infrequent it is. It is the same principle that creates an addiction to slot machines. Getting a winner only occasionally motivates you

Texting Tips for Parents

- Carefully evaluate the age of your kids when they start texting on their cell phones. Just because other kids in their class have it doesn't mean your child needs it.
- If your kids do text, get an unlimited texting plan. Otherwise the charges mount up swiftly.
- Make rules around when and where. No texting during meals, during class, on family outings. Oh, and turn the phone OFF at night!
- No texting while they should be concentrating on something else. This includes driving—nearly half of teens admit to texting while driving—walking, and having a conversation with someone else. Firm rules about this will ensure their safety as well as their social skills.
- Establish consequences for misuse. Cheating, inappropriate messages, sexual communication. These are all no-go's. Want to make your point? Take your kid's phone away for a week.
- Watch your own behavior. Parents are still models for their kids. If you text your child while they are in class and then turn around and tell that child that he or she can't text in class, you're sending mixed signals.
- If you suspect your kids aren't texting appropriately, you can always look at their messages. Yes, it feels like snooping, but our first job as parents is to ensure that our kids use powerful technologies safely and responsibly.[8]

to keep trying to win. Casinos know this and make fortunes in the process! Receiving an occasional exciting message "hit" creates a greater addiction than getting exciting messages all the time. It is this form of "intermittent reinforcement" that makes texting an addictive behavior, because the anticipation of not knowing when you will get a "good hit" is why you get hooked.

While becoming hooked on texting or instant messaging may not seem to be a serious addiction, it is a problem that can consume a lot of time, interfering with work, studying, homework, and healthy social interactions. The statistics keep changing, but presently the surge in text messaging is mainly by teens between the ages of thirteen and seventeen years. They send and receive on average about 3,339 text messages a month. Teens also talk on the phone, but at a much lower rate, using around 646 minutes talking on the phone per month. The report even suggests that kids under the age of twelve are now also becoming heavy texters, averaging about 1,146 messages per month.[9]

This is a digital activity that parents can easily overlook. Texting provides a cheap and easy way to stay in touch with friends. It is also a time waster; so parents need to set limits on when and how long their children can text and make sure their children are not texting at inappropriate times of the day. Texting can easily become a major disrupter of school or other important activities. Our experience is that many teenagers do their texting in the early hours of the morning when they should be getting some rejuvenating sleep.

How Addicted Are You or Your Children?

"How can you tell whether your children have some form of Internet addiction?" is the most common question parents ask us in our seminars. Many suspect their children may have a problem but are not sure whether they, or their children, or both, are in trouble.

Let us begin by describing some general symptoms of Internet addiction. Look carefully at the following list and see how many of the characteristics are present in your life or your children's lives:

SYMPTOMS OF INTERNET ADDICTION

- There is a heightened sense of euphoria whenever they are involved in Internet activities.
- There is a general neglect of friends and family, and priority given to Internet activity.
- They have tried several times to cut back on Internet usage but have failed in their attempts to control behavior.
- They suffer from serious sleep deprivation because they engage the Internet well into the night.
- They develop a general style of dishonesty and increasingly engage in denial.
- Physical changes are noticeable, such as an increase in stress, weight gain or loss, backaches, headaches, high blood pressure, gastric or other health problems.
- They withdraw from all real-life activities that were once pleasurable, giving priority to some form of digital engagement.
- They may have feelings of guilt, shame, anxiety, or depression that are the result of excess online behavior.

There are many Internet addiction tests available on the Internet. (We know that seems ironic.) But we provide you with our simple test to give you an idea of how attached to the Internet you or your teenager have become. If you suspect an addiction problem or have any serious concern, consult a professional with expertise in this area.

Teenage Digital Addiction Test

Instructions: Because your teenager might downplay the seriousness of their problem, we recommend you work through the test yourself and answer the questions as they apply to your teenager. Score your teenager's response to each question using the following ratings:

   0—Never or rarely.

   1—Occasionally (seems to be able to control it).

   2—Often (several times a week, but for a long time).

   3—Always (every day, and for a lot of the time).

SCORE

____ 1. Your teenager neglects household chores in order to go on the Internet.

____ 2. Your teenager prefers to be on the Internet rather than play with friends.

____ 3. Getting your teenager to stop his/her computer activity in order to come to dinner or some family activity is difficult.

____ 4. Your teenager's interactions with friends are mainly via the Internet.

____ 5. Spending time on the Internet is clearly having a detrimental effect on your teenager's grades.

____ 6. The time spent on the Internet is clearly having a detrimental effect on your teenager's relationships with friends and family.

____ 7. Your teenager loses sleep because he or she spends time on the Internet.

____ 8. Your teenager appears to be depressed or moody, but cheers up when using the Internet.

____ 9. When the computer is down or cell phone not working, or you restrict usage, your teenager becomes moody, irritable, or angry.

____ 10. Your teenager appears unable to really enjoy anything that does not involve the Internet.

_____ TOTAL SCORE

Interpreting the score:

   10 or below: Your teenager does not appear to be addicted and is able to exercise appropriate control.

   11 to 20: Your teenager may be experiencing occasional "dependence" on the Internet and may be showing signs of a growing addiction.

   21 to 30: Your teenager may be addicted to some aspect of the Internet. Seek professional help in making a determination.

Adult Digital Addiction Test

Instructions: Use the following scale to enter your score for each question:

    0—Never or rarely.

    1—Occasionally (seems to be able to control it).

    2—Often (several times a week, but for a long time).

    3—Always (every day, and for a lot of the time).

SCORE

_____ 1. You use and stay on the Internet longer than you intend to when you sit down in front of your computer.

_____ 2. Your work suffers from how much time you spend on the Internet.

_____ 3. How often does your spouse or someone else complain that you spend too much time on the Internet?

_____ 4. How often do you neglect or forget your chores or other duties because you are spending time on the Internet?

_____ 5. You become defensive whenever anyone asks you what it is you are doing on the Internet.

_____ 6. How often is your sleep affected by your being on the Internet? (Because it robs you of sleep or you cannot get to sleep)

_____ 7. During the day, do you spend time thinking about or find yourself anticipating when you will be able to get on the Internet?

_____ 8. How often do you get mad when someone bothers you when you are on the Internet?

_____ 9. When your computer or the Internet is "down," do you get angry or upset to the point where others can see it?

_____ 10. Do you tend to check your email compulsively—i.e., more frequently than is necessary?

_____ 11. Do you feel that you prefer the excitement of the Internet to the intimacy you can enjoy with your partner, spouse, or friends?

_____ 12. Do you find that while you say to yourself, "I'll stop now," you continue working on the device?

_____ 13. Do you find that when you are sad, down, anxious, or moody, going on the Internet lifts your mood?

_____ 14. If you had to choose between the Internet and any other social activity, how often would you choose the Internet?

_____ 15. Do you find that you now have more friends or contacts on the Internet than you do in real life?

_____ TOTAL SCORE

Interpreting the score:

    10 or below: Doubtful that you have any Internet addiction.

    11 to 20: You have the beginnings of addiction and may be more hooked than you realize.

    21 to 30: It is clear that you are addicted to some aspects of the Internet, and it may be doing harm to your social and personal life.

    Over 30: Your Internet addiction is severe enough that you should consider getting professional help for overcoming it.

Overcoming an Internet Addiction

The treatment level for Internet Addiction Disorder is considered difficult because going cold turkey is impossible when our digital use impacts every aspect of our business and social life. Research has shown the most effective treatment plan for overcoming digital addiction is Cognitive Behavioral Therapy.[10] This treatment is based on the premise that thoughts determine feelings. This model helps explain how negative self-thoughts can fuel the compulsive behavior associated with the digital addiction. The most common negative emotions present in those with digital addictions are depression and anxiety. The other emotions digital addicts feel are being tense, lonely, restless, withdrawn, angry, or useless.[11]

In treating digital addictions, the goal is to abstain from the application you are most addicted to while using the other needed digital applications moderately.

Digital Addiction Treatment Plan

1. **Reduce stress.** Our connection addiction is stressing us out, and stress causes anxiety.
2. **Deal with anxiety.** The more anxious we become, the more we reach for our digital gadgets to manage our anxiety.
3. **Limit use of addictive digital applications.** Going cold turkey isn't reasonable as our lives are so intertwined in the digital world. Set boundaries on the most addictive applications.
4. **Replace negative thinking.** Excessive digital use can reinforce low self-esteem and depression. Counterbalance with real activities; change the way you think—be more positive.
5. **Reclaim real-life relationships.** One of the cores of recovery is to learn new ways to connect and relate to others. Cultivate face-to-face conversations and limit digital interactions.
6. **Establish an accountability partner.** The most successful recovery programs incorporate support from others around us; we really do need each other to overcome.
7. **Access online resources:**
   Overcoming Digital Addictions Workbook by Dr. Sylvia Hart Frejd and Dr. Archibald Hart, www.TheDigitalInvasion.com
   Recovery Programs for Internet Addiction:
   Restart Addiction Recovery, www.netaddictionrecovery.com
   Tech Addiction, www.techaddiction.ca
   The Center for Counseling and Health, www.aplaceofhope.com

What We Can Do about It

If you know someone with a digital addiction, the following are some suggestions that you can use to help them toward recovery:

- Be a good role model. Manage your own digital life well.
- Introduce the digital addict to other people who handle their digital life sensibly.
- Get your friend or loved one involved in nondigital interests.
- Talk to them about your concerns over their digital use.
- Support their desire for change if they think they have a problem.
- Encourage them to seek professional help.

If you are struggling with your own Internet addiction, here are suggestions for your own recovery:

- Find someone who can serve as an accountability partner for you. If you have several friends who are also addicted, start a support group which can offer tremendous assistance and challenge you when you stray.
- Unlike drug addictions, you really cannot abandon all your Internet connections, so determine what the minimum amount of Internet activity is necessary in your life and make that your goal. Your spouse may have some suggestions, or your support group could agree together on what limits you should set.
- Set aside specific times, and lengths of time, you want to be on the Internet.
- Keep a detailed log so you can track your usage and hold yourself accountable.
- Delete Internet sites and apps from your computer or smartphone that you do not need or that are too tempting. There are scores of Internet businesses that will plug their site into your computer in some way; keep track of them.
- Develop non-Internet hobbies to occupy your free time, like reading real books, bicycling, joining an exercise group, knitting, or woodworking.

- If you really find it a struggle to break your addiction, seek out a counselor. There may be other issues that underlie your addiction.

- As a Christian believer, make your recovery a matter of prayer. We are not alone in our personal struggles. God has offered us help in many ways. (Check out 2 Chron. 16:9 and Isa. 40:28–31.)

Alcoholics Anonymous and many other recovery groups have adopted the following prayer—it's called "The Serenity Prayer." Consider using this prayer regularly as you seek to overcome your addiction. Reflect on what this simple prayer means and how you can live the real life God wants you to live.

The Serenity Prayer

God, give us grace to accept with serenity
the things that cannot be changed,
Courage to change the things
which should be changed,
and the wisdom to distinguish
the one from the other.

Living one day at a time,
Enjoying one moment at a time,
Accepting hardship as a pathway to peace,
Taking, as Jesus did, this sinful world as it is,
Not as I would have it,
Trusting that You will make all things right,
If I surrender to Your will,
So that I may be reasonably happy in this life,
And supremely happy with You forever in the next.
Amen.

                                        Reinhold Niebuhr

Discussion Questions

1. Do you believe that people can form Internet or digital addictions? Share why or why not.

2. Have you experienced any of the consequences of Internet addiction described in this chapter?

3. Share what you have learned about how Internet addictions are formed that was helpful to you.

4. How did you and your family score on the test for internet addictions? Discuss what you are going to do about it if anyone was out of bounds, or what you can do to prevent addictions in your family.

5. Which of the steps to breaking your internet addiction outlined in this chapter are you ready to take?

6. As you read the Serenity Prayer at the end of the chapter, which part of the prayer do you find the most challenging?

8

Intentional Living in a Digital World

So be careful how you act; these are difficult days. Don't be fools; be wise: make the most of every opportunity you have for doing good. Don't act thoughtlessly, but try to find out and do whatever the Lord wants you to.

Ephesians 5:15–17 TLB

A few years ago pastor and author John Piper wrote a book entitled *Don't Waste Your Life*. We would like to expand Piper's phrase in this chapter to "*Don't Waste Your* Real *Life* on a virtual life." The life the Internet is invading and overtaking is our "real life." There is a growing concern among mental health professionals, neuroscientists, and church leaders that using our digital technology to the extreme is tantamount to wasting our real life away. Not only is the cyber world changing our brains, as we showed in chapter 3, it is changing our behavior, manners, culture, and customs. As our title to this chapter suggests, we need to be intentional in how we live our digital lives. We need to be intentional in the choices we make and the systems we adopt, and be careful not to waste our lives away on useless busywork and the barren pursuits of what a lot of digital technology offers us.

Our world is changing rapidly, which means we cannot ignore the consequences of overusing the cyber world. We must be calculated in what we do if we want to achieve the highest level of well-being and fulfill God's plan for our lives. Intentional living is about thriving and being responsible for the choices that shape our lives. This includes not spending excessive amounts of time being consumed by, and roaming around, the digital world. Unfortunately too many are already living *The Pointless Driven Life* and not *The Purpose Driven Life* that Rick Warren wrote about in his bestselling book.

This Digital Invasion Chart below illustrates how consumption of technological media has increased over the last ten years. It will probably be out of date by the time this book is published, but it gives you some idea of how invasive digital technology has become. We now spend eighteen hours or more a week online, searching Google two billion times every day, and spend four hours a day on Facebook. Much of this time we are spending is pointless.

The Digital Invasion Chart

In 2000	In 2013
Spent 2.7 hours per week online	Spent more than 30 hours per week online[1]
100 million daily Google searches	4.7 billion daily Google searches[2]
14 billion text messages sent daily	188 billion text messages sent daily[3]
0 apps downloaded	25 billion apps downloaded[4]
0 YouTube video monthly views	Over 800 million YouTube monthly views[5]
0 people on Facebook	1 billion people on Facebook[6]
0 Tweets on Twitter	400 million tweets per day on Twitter[7]

In working as a life coach, my (Dr. Frejd's) job is to help people find and fulfill their potential. I am concerned that life in the digital world can become a threat to this potential. I spoke recently with a young man we will call Charlie, a college student, who is bright, very smart, and dreams of becoming a doctor someday and making a difference in this world. He shared his problem with me. Charlie is addicted to video gaming. He told me he spends eight to nine hours a day playing them. He admits he is totally hooked and is getting D's and F's in his classes. He is not happy and wants to stop, but says that he can't. I fear there are too many "Charlies" out there who have grand goals and dreams, but risk never realizing them because of this distractive digital activity.

Maybe for you it's not gaming that is invading your real life and holding you back, but Googling, Facebook, or other smartphone apps. Unless you learn how to steward your technology, you may live with unfulfilled goals and dreams. So our message is this: *Don't let your virtual life rob you of your real life.* You are not here by accident. You are not on this earth merely to live out a certain number of days, and then die. You are here to accomplish a job that God has assigned to you. God has a purpose, a plan, and a destination for your life, but it will take great intent and discipline on your part to follow this path. We want to offer hope so that you can reclaim what the digital invasion has already stolen from your life. Every digital user needs to pay attention to how much they use technology. It comes down to a simple matter of time spent and the intensity with which you engage your digital world.

How Digitally Engaged Are You?

As a counselor and coach, I (Dr. Frejd) hear clients many times say, "How did I get to this place in my life?" My answer to them is always the same: "The path you chose brought you here, so you will have to choose another path to take you where you need to be." Your intentions determine your direction; the path you choose determines where you end up. This is an opportunity for you to evaluate where you are in your digital engagement and intentionally choose the path you need to take to ensure a healthy outcome.

These are truly desperate times we are living in. We are spending less time moving our bodies, enjoying ourselves in nature, and cultivating healthy relationships. Stress, anxiety, and depression related disorders are on the rise. People are struggling with being more isolated and disconnected. We have already talked about the "dumbing down" of our brain capacity. What do we have to show for all the time spent pointlessly in the digital world? Could this time have been spent practicing an instrument, reading a great book, playing a sport, or enjoying nature?

In chapter 7 we discussed what having a full-blown digital addiction looks like, but even if you don't fall into the "addicted" group, you may still be overusing your digital engagement. Take a look at the list of digital applications below and circle those you could be overusing:

Smartphone apps	Gaming	iPod
iPad	Pinterest	Instagram
Googling	Email	Texting
Internet	Social media (Facebook, Twitter, LinkedIn, etc.)	
Other (describe) _____		

Dealing with overuse of digital technology starts by being honest with yourself and staying aware of which of the digital applications you are overusing. Take the "Digital Use Assessment Quiz" to evaluate how you are doing.

Digital Use Assessment Quiz

Answer yes or no

____ 1. Do you text and drive even though you know it's not the safe thing to do?

____ 2. Do you get the urge to use your smartphone when someone else is talking to you?

____ 3. Do you ever feel something hasn't really happened until you post it on Facebook?

____ 4. Does your family sit in the same room but not talk to each other because you are all interacting with your digital gadgets?

____ 5. Do you find a ringing or vibrating cell phone interrupts and trumps everything else?

____ 6. Do you ever lie about your Internet or online gaming use?

____ 7. Are you experiencing a loss of interest in other activities you used to enjoy?

____ 8. Do you neglect yourself (sleeping/eating) because of time spent in the digital world?

____ 9. Do you feel anxious if you are offline for a period of time?

____ 10. Do you ever think about how you could focus better in real life without all these gadgets invading your space?

____ Number of yes answers.

Interpreting the score:

0: Perfect score. You are doing very well in managing your digital world.

1 to 3: Your digital usage is good.

4 to 6: You have a problem, so caution is needed.

7 to 10: Your digital engagement is excessive, so take immediate steps to bring it under control.

Guarding Your Well-Being

Research coming out of the "Positive Psychology" movement, a new approach to preventing emotional problems, has shown that about 50 percent of our positive emotional states, like happiness, hopefulness, and contentment, are influenced by our genetics. Only 10 percent

of these positive emotions are determined by our circumstances, and
the remaining 40 percent is "up to us."[8] Dr. Catherine Hart Weber,
my (Dr. Frejd's) sister, has written a book entitled *Flourish: Discover
the Daily Joy of Abundant, Vibrant Living*, in which she lays out how
God has created us, and provided us with what we need to flourish
in our lives.[9] Unfortunately, many today are not flourishing in their
lives, but languishing. Statistics indicate that only about 18 percent
of people meet the criteria for "flourishing well," while 17 percent are
languishing. Others fall somewhere in between.[10] Millions of dollars
are being spent on research and developing interventions that focus on
how we can reduce misery and prevent languishing, while enhancing
our happiness and the quality of life. We are sorry to report that not a
lot of attention is being given to exploring where our over-engagement
of the digital world fits into all of this.

Dr. Weber goes on to explain flourishing this way: "You flourish when
your life has meaning and purpose and you routinely experience emotion
virtues such as love, joy, gratitude, peace, and hope. We have meaning
when we know we are making a positive impact on the lives of others
around us through our work and legacy."[11] Intentionally cultivating these
areas of our life will guard against the depletion of our pleasure center.
Our brain is hardwired for love, joy, peace, and hope, and it is God's plan

Estimated Current Digital Use

Please state the approximate number of hours you engage in the following activities. The individual activities should approximately equal the
total number of hours spent online for recreational purposes or gaming.
    Note: Provide estimates for a typical week

Estimated Weekly Hours

Video games	___	Reading news	___
Chatting online	___	Reading blogs	___
Shopping (non-auction)	___	Email	___
eBay	___	Gathering information	___
Facebook/MySpace/Instagram	___	Pinterest	___
Downloading music	___	Viewing pornography	___
Downloading videos	___	Watching videos (e.g., YouTube)	___
Listening to Podcasts	___	Message boards / newsgroups	___
"Playing" with software	___	Twitter	___

Total estimated weekly hours ___

for us to discover authentic joy and pure, good pleasures for our lives. We are not likely to achieve this level of flourishing through our digital world because it plays havoc with our pleasure center. We have to be intentional in protecting, as well as recovering, a healthy pleasure system.

It is in this context that we want you to ask yourself this question: How does my use of technology contribute to my happiness and well-being, and how does it hinder?

Your flourishing and well-being can be enhanced or hindered by how you use your media and technology. Throughout our book, we have emphasized that it is not the technology itself that determines whether we flourish or languish, but rather how we use it. Albert Einstein once remarked, "Why does this magnificent applied science which saves work and makes life easier bring us so little happiness?" He asked this question long before the discovery of digital technology, but it is still very applicable. Applying it to our digital world, the simple answer is, because we have not yet learned to make sensible use of it. What matters is that we remain intentional, balanced, sensible, and fully aware of the impact that technology can have on our overall well-being.

In order to flourish in well-being, we must be intentional in managing our physical, spiritual, emotional, relational, and now, our virtual life. Your virtual life is an added dimension to your being that will be with you for the rest of your time here on earth.

Five Ways to Restore Your Pleasure Center

- *Live a connected life.* Nurture your relationships. Healthy, loving relationship connections are the most important predictor of present and future happiness, health, well-being, and longevity.
- *Aim for sovereign joy.* God's joy in us can be learned. Find joy in the simple things, a baby's smile, or a hug from a friend. Be a joy spreader as well.
- *Receive God's peace.* God offers the gift of his peace as the antidote to the stress in our "always-on" life. Calm your mind and body and be aware of what steals your peace.
- *Practice gratitude.* Having a grateful heart leads to a healthier body, a happier mind, and relationships that flourish. Gratitude is the healthiest emotion for your brain and, in turn, your life. So count your blessings every day.
- *Cultivate hope and resilience.* Keep the changes of life in perspective. When one door closes, look for God to open another one. Have a vision of God's purpose and plan for your life. Find tangible ways to stay motivated.

Every digital gadget demands careful monitoring and intentional boundary setting if you are going to prevent it from negatively affecting many aspects of your life.

Establishing Digital Boundaries

Clinical psychologist and blogger Doreen Dodgen-Magee says this about our digital intake: "I was looking through some old *Life* magazines from the '50s one night and noticed that all the ads were for convenience foods and cigarettes. It hit me that by the '70s, or about 15 to 20 years into us becoming completely enamored with convenience foods and cigarettes, we find out about lung cancer and we have the FDA coming out with this food pyramid suggesting that, oops, maybe the high fat and high sodium in convenience foods weren't such a great idea. And that's what I think about technology. We so embrace this thing that could be a wonderful side dish or accompaniment to our lives. But it's become the main event. What are we going to see in 10 to 15 years that will be too late to control?"[12]

The sheer volume of what is available for us to consume through the Internet is overwhelming. This plethora of information and engagement is not only making it difficult for us to flourish, but it is also taking a toll on our health. In the United States, where two-thirds of the people are now overweight, none of these people woke up one day and said, "I think I will eat poorly and get really fat." In the 1970s, manufacturers intentionally started making food with all kinds of sweeteners and artificial ingredients that were designed to make us crave junk food. This high-calorie food was designed to be alluring and tempting. It was also big business. We can also say this about our current digital engagement. Just like with food, we must take responsibility for our use of technology and try to assemble the lifestyle changes that are needed to prevent us from going too far down the digital-damage road. We need to educate, inform, persuade, and coach people about what is truly healthy and best for them. Our need for a digital diet is similar to our need for a food diet. We all have to eat, and we all will ingest technology in some form or another. Just as we need to take great care in our food diet, we need to take great care in our digital diet, using technology in a way that has healthy benefits on our lives. We don't have to stuff ourselves at the all-you-can-eat digital buffet.

So what is the proper use of food? Food is for nourishment, fellowship, and celebration. What is the proper use of digital technology? It is to make life easier and more convenient, for obtaining the information we need to connect socially with others, and yes, also for entertainment.

These are some questions you need to ask yourself about your digital diet:

1. Is digital technology helping to make my life easier, or is it making it harder?
2. Is all my searching and Googling for long periods healthy for my life?
3. Is technology helping me to connect on a deeper level with those I love?
4. Is my time spent on entertainment being managed well?

Borrowing from how the dietary world explains our food diet, let us look at the following diagram illustrating *our current digital diet* use in this pyramid:[13]

Figure 3

The Current Digital Diet Pyramid

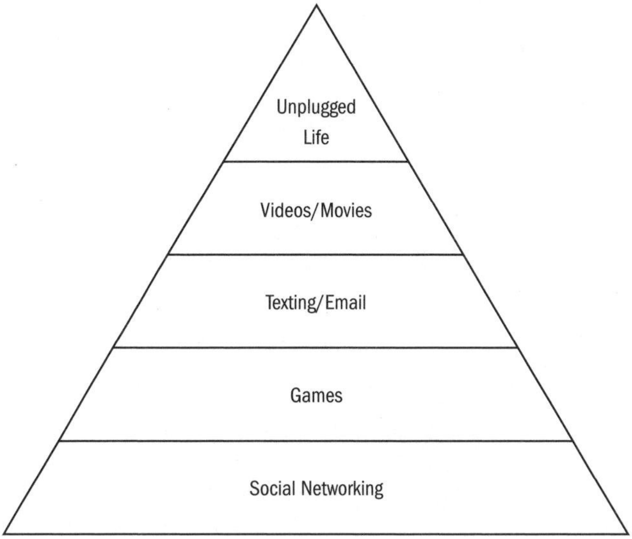

- Unplugged Life
- Videos/Movies
- Texting/Email
- Games
- Social Networking

As you can see, the typical "Current Digital Diet" shows that we spend most of our time online socially networking. Then comes entertainment like games, followed by texting and emailing. The least amount of our time is spent being unplugged.

Our digital life serves us best when it is balanced by its opposite—namely, our unplugged life. In fact, if you turn your current digital diet pyramid upside down, your diet would be healthier. We need to spend the most time unplugged and in real life as we can. This is true for our whole family, not just for adults. While we should use our technologies for their intended purposes, we should also find time for doing real-life things.

Now let us use the following blank pyramid and design our own diet:

Figure 4

Design Your Own Digital Diet Pyramid

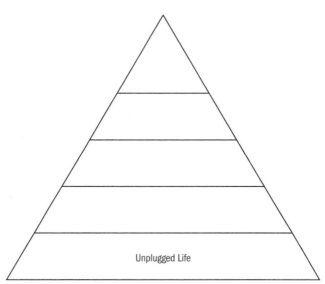

Notice that your "Unplugged Life" is now at the bottom, taking up most of your time. This is imperative if you want maximum health from your digital diet. Now take the time to fill in the rest of your digital diet pyramid above with how you would like to manage your digital life. Then we suggest you make a photocopy of your pyramid and paste it somewhere in your home or at work to remind you of your digital diet. Follow it as conscientiously as you do your food diet.

You can also make some blank pyramids for other family members to fill out as well.

I (Dr. Frejd) wanted to share some of the digital boundaries that I have set up for myself and hope they will encourage you in establishing your own digital boundaries.

MY DIGITAL BOUNDARIES

• Do not check my smartphone until after my morning devotions.

• Try to end my digital day by 9:00 p.m.

• Don't check my smartphone when having lunch or dinner with a friend, or leave phone in car.

• Take a digital fast every Sunday.

• No digital gadgets at mealtimes.

• Limit checking emails or texts to once an hour.

• Try not to talk on the phone to virtual people when real people are in front of me.

• Pray daily for God to help me become a good steward of my virtual life.

Intentional Strategies to Help You Thrive in Your Real Life

I (Dr. Frejd) came across a new app recently. Its title? SelfControl.[14] The website explains that if you lack self-control when you are on the Internet, you can easily download some self-control from this app.[15] What a novel idea! The SelfControl app can block access to all kinds of activities that are intrusive, like mail servers, social media, and other websites. The great thing about this app is that you can block one or two websites you find distracting, but still have access to the rest of the web. This may be a helpful app, but what we really need in our digital diet is more practical self-control, not just an app. A prompting from the Holy Spirit would serve us better. We don't like to tell ourselves no or to delay gratification. Studies have shown us that self-controlled individuals are more adept than their impulsive counterparts at regulating their behavioral, emotional, and attentional impulses to achieve long-term goals. We all need boundaries and clear limits, just like the psalmist who said, "Like a city whose walls are broken through is a person who lacks self-control" (Prov. 25:28). To restrain our appetites brings us great gain, because it builds in us the reserves that we need when we are tempted to cross a boundary we will later regret. In ancient times, a city without walls was vulnerable to an enemy who wanted to invade and attack. In the same way, a life that does not cultivate boundaries, or to use the psalmist's language, "strong walls," is also vulnerable to any digital invasion or distraction that comes its way. You cannot indulge in little weaknesses and assume they will not eventually take over and weaken your whole life. Anything left out of control will weaken your life.

A great way to establish healthy boundaries with your digital intake is to find a reasonable time each day that marks the end of your "e-day" where you turn everything off and use no electronics unless it's an emergency. Try to end your e-day no later than 9:00 p.m. and take a break or do some exercise. Darken your environment and minimize the noise and stress from technology by setting your smartphones to vibrate and turn down the volume on your laptop and any alerts or alarms.

Ten Steps to Digital Well-Being

1. Think twice before you post or tweet it.
2. Share your Facebook user name and password with your spouse.
3. Take a digital fast once a week or once a month.
4. Practice the presence of people—real people trump virtual people.
5. Evaluate whether you really need a new digital gadget before purchasing it.
6. Spend as much time in your real life as you can.
7. Model good digital stewardship to your family.
8. Sleep device free. Keep the phones out of the bedroom (or at least on Silent!).
9. Daily cultivate your "Godspace." (See chap. 10.)
10. Sanctify your technology and use it for God's glory.

Where Have All Our Manners Gone?

In our fast-paced society with its multiple demands, there is a real danger that we are losing our manners, especially our social etiquette. Home manners go missing as family activities become digitally interrupted. Hospitality wanes as distractions spread us thin. With the anonymity afforded by the Internet, the comments section of blog posts and newspaper websites teem with discourteous discussion.

Consequently, it is important that we be more intentional in using common courtesies. Graciousness and kindness are an integral part of courteous behavior. Graciousness is the ability to make other people feel welcome and comfortable in your world. Kindness is much like consideration, but it also reflects the warmth in your heart. To be civil and courteous is the outward expression of Christlikeness. Human decency is more important than ever in today's complex and changing digital world.

No doubt you have observed what I (Dr. Frejd) am about to describe and can share many similar stories yourself. A young couple in their late twenties was seated at a restaurant table next to me. The young man cradled his smartphone, 100 percent engrossed in that tiny computer screen. This went on for forty-five minutes while his date was seated across from him. She, in her boredom, started to play with her cell phone also. Soon the two of them were spending more time on their phones than with each other. The meal ended with hardly a word spoken to each other.

This may seem trivial, but events like this are happening in restaurants and homes all around us. "Smartphone fidgeting" seems to be the new dating style. The phenomenon has been coined *absent presence*, meaning that someone uses their phone to check their messages, play video games, or play with apps while they are with someone else. It is because of this out-of-control digital behavior that we would like to start our own "Netiquette Revolution." We are calling it "BE WHERE YOUR BUTT IS." We like this phrase, as it aptly describes what is needed. How many times have you found yourself sitting with someone in a room, yet in conversation with someone not in your presence? Instead of "absent presence," we would suggest that you practice "present presence."

This revolution is about practicing the presence of people. When you find yourself in this situation, hit the pause on your smartphone or close your laptop, and reconnect with whoever is present. As an example, if you are having lunch with a friend or your spouse, try to stay focused, present, and in the moment with each person. Give them your full attention. Put your smartphone on vibrate and keep it in your purse or pocket. Resist the urge to check it. Better yet, leave it in your car. If you are checking out at Wal-Mart, engage the clerk that is ringing you up. Say, "Hello, how is your day going?" Or "You are doing a great job!" Another idea is to make a "no heads down" rule in your home where there is no looking down at a computer or cell phone during a conversation. If the person does not take the time to look you in the eye, stop the conversation until they do. Wouldn't it be amazing if we all would "be where our butt is"?

We also want to present some basic etiquette rules. In South Korea, they call it *netiquette* and have instigated a program nationwide to train their schoolchildren in how to show etiquette on the Internet. In time we believe it will spread to other countries as well, because everyone needs a little netiquette. The Golden Rule of Netiquette is to *do unto others on the Internet as you would have done to you.*

Ten Core Rules of Internet Netiquette

1. Try to be polite and respectful at all times.
2. Spell-check and proofread everything you send, because errors diminish the credibility of the message.
3. Don't use all caps, because all caps are considered to be shouting.
4. Tell the truth online and in your profiles, because honesty creates the best online experience. But be careful and only reveal what is appropriate.
5. Don't do things online you wouldn't do in real life. Be yourself—you are not anonymous.
6. Don't explode or respond in some nasty way, because personal insults are uncivilized and netiquette is civilized.
7. Don't follow spam or pop-up links, because they can lead to viruses and spyware.
8. Be conservative in email you send, because quality is better than quantity.
9. Don't make it a habit to FB, email, or tweet in the late-night hours.
10. Use discretion when sharing information online for personal and professional reasons.[16]

Setting Intentional Limits on Technology

In a 2011 Barna survey, parents and teens were asked if they had times when they personally made the choice to disconnect from or turn off technology to take a break from it. Of the parents surveyed, 67 percent said they take a break from technology, and 33 percent said they do not.[17]

Of the teens surveyed, 56 percent said they take a break and 44 percent said they do not take breaks. Parents need to work on taking breaks and need to help their teens be more intentional to take breaks as well. One mom told us that she keeps all the family's iPhones and laptops on a table in her living/dining room in the evenings, when her family tends to hang out together. She said, "I try, but don't always succeed, to make it clear to my kids that there is a value on focusing on one thing at a time. I think I'm more aware of what we're all doing; when I walk into a room and see everyone looking at a screen, I call their attention to the fact we're all looking at screens instead of each other."

Figure 5
Decisions to Disconnect from Technology

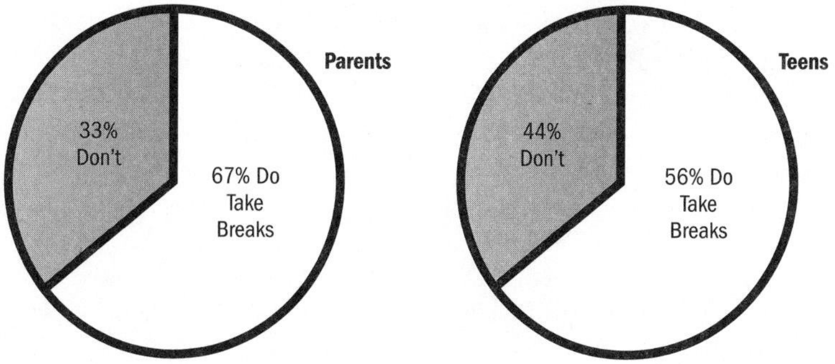

Parents

33% Don't

67% Do Take Breaks

Teens

44% Don't

56% Do Take Breaks

The Digital Fast Challenge

A few years ago, my (Dr. Frejd's) life coach encouraged me to unplug on my upcoming vacation. I remember thinking to myself, "There is no way that's going to happen!" At the last minute I decided to take her advice and reluctantly left my laptop at home and didn't use my cell phone at all. After a few days of "digital detoxing," I experienced the best vacation I have ever had. I was so relaxed and connected with my family that when I came home I didn't want to plug back in again.

Would you be able to abstain from technology for a weekend? Could you restrict your Internet use or Facebook checking for twenty-four hours? Or does the sound of this nearly give you a panic attack! The fact is that anything we can't fast from owns us. The value of this kind of digital fasting and disconnecting is tremendously important for our physical health, our soul, and our spirit. As with food fasting, digital fasting breaks the habitual patterns that we fall into so easily. It will make your brain more flexible and more able to do creative work. More importantly, it will make you more aware of any addictions you may have and change what you are doing with the people and situations around you.

As part of this book project, we are promoting a worldwide campaign called *The Digital Fast Challenge*, inviting people to regularly unplug from all their digital gadgets for twenty-four hours and plug into their real life. One student had this to say before trying the fast: "I figure I can do it and it won't be that hard. And if it is that hard, I'll probably have to reevaluate my relationship with these things. I want to prove to myself, as I think I will, that they are an addition to my life, not an addiction." Unplugging and taking a digital fast will not only make a difference in your life, but it will help you determine whether technology is an addition to your life, or an addiction.

We have begun to present this Digital Fast Challenge at universities, churches, military bases, and conferences around the country. Below are some of the responses of those who have taken the challenge and fasted from their technology:

- "It was an unpleasant surprise to realize that I am in a state of constant distraction, as if my real life and my virtual life were coexisting in different planes, but in equal time."
- "It was amazing to me how easily programmed my fingers are to instantly type F-A-C-E in the search bar. It's now muscle memory, or instinctual, to log into Facebook as the first step of Internet browsing."
- "I've lived with the same people for 3 years now, they're my best friends, and I think that this is one of the best days we've spent together, I was able to really see them, without any distractions, and we were able to revert to simple pleasures."
- "Media has put us close to the people who are far away but has separated us from the ones who are nearby."

In contrast to our calling for a "digital fast," a recent article on CNN.com tells of a prominent blogger who is not thinking of a fast for a day or two but is taking a whole year's sabbatical. He states:

"I've been on the Internet for the majority of hours of my waking life. I just want to know how it's impacting me and the parts of it that might not be good for me."[18] We are not necessarily advocating you detach yourself from the digital world for a whole year, but it is very clear from this prominent blogger's perspective that periodically detaching from all digital engagements can be a healthy thing. We believe the same, and encourage you to step back and take a digital fast periodically.

One pastor shared recently that a man came up to him at church and asked if he had received his email. The pastor inquired, "Did you send it before Friday morning?" The man replied, "I sent it on Friday." But the pastor has decided to make Friday and Saturday his "fasting days off," and this includes NOT checking emails on his smartphone because that is part of his work. The best he could do without offending the church member was to assure him, "I'll get to your email Monday morning."

This pastor is being very intentional in managing his smartphone and not allowing it to manage him, and church members need to respect this action. Telling them, "I'm not checking emails Friday through Sunday, and will resume on Monday morning. They will still be there," is a perfect example of smart usage of his smartphone. He uses and enjoys all the benefits and apps of his phone, but has learned how to steward it well.

What We Can Do about It

Now it's your turn. We invite you to join our challenge and take a twenty-four-hour digital fast to unplug from digital technology and plug into your real life for one day a week, or one day a month. Try to take it on a Saturday or a Sunday, turn off your computer, iPad, and smartphone. We know your emails will pile up if you don't look at them for a day or two, but you will be amazed at how much easier it will be to deal with them after taking a day off.

Instead of using your Kindle, read a regular book and underline in it and write in the margin. Instead of typing, write with pen and paper. Living intentionally in this digital world means you will need to awaken to your relationship with technology, assess what it is that technology has stolen from you, and then reclaim your real life and real relationships.

After you have taken your first digital fast, let us know how it went. We look forward to hearing about your digital fasting story at our website, www.TheDigitalInvasion.com or on www.Facebook.com/ TheDigitalFastChallenge.

Figure 6

The Digital Fast Challenge

UNPLUGGED

A challenge to unplug and fast from digital technology for 24 hours and to plug into your real life

The Purpose:

AWAKEN to your relationship with technology
ASSESS what technology has stolen from you
RECLAIM your real life and real relationships

Unplug from all digital technology and plug into God's Word.
Spend time with Him in silence and solitude and then connect with your real-life relationships.

Share your unplugged story with us:
www.TheDigitalInvasion.com
Facebook.com/TheDigitalFastChallenge

Discussion Questions

1. How did you score on the "Digital Use Assessment Quiz"?

2. Have you spent much time thinking about the healthy uses of digital technology? Explain.

3. Which suggestions from the "Ten Steps to Digital Well-Being" would you like to implement?

4. Would you like to be a part of the "Be Where Your Butt Is" Revolution? If so, how will you do that?

5. Discuss which of the "Ten Core Rules of Netiquette" that were most helpful to you.

6. Would you like to participate in "The Digital Fast Challenge"? Share how you are going to make that happen.

9

A Parent's Digital
Protection Plan

And so . . . I plead with you to give your bodies to God. Let
them be a living sacrifice, holy—the kind he can accept. . . .
Don't copy the behavior and customs of this world, but
be a new and different person with a fresh newness in all
you do and think.

Romans 12:1–2 TLB

They watch it. They listen to it. They download from it. They connect
to it. They play on it and surf on it. And they certainly converse with
it. But do you, as a parent, have any idea what percentage of your
children's daily life is taken up with it? "It" is, of course, one or more
of the applications the digital natives play with. Do you know how
to monitor and discipline your children's usage? It can be challenging
and demanding for parents to keep up with all the digital gadgets, but
if we want our children to stay safe in this digital world, it's crucial
that we do all we can to protect them.

Let's take a look at a typical young boy. We'll call him Trey. His
mother had him watch all the "Baby Einstein" videos. I (Dr. Hart)
suspect that some older readers, like myself, have never heard of Baby
Einstein, a line of multimedia products like videos and toys, made by
Disney, that specialize in interactive activities for children aged three

months to three or four years. Well, by the time Trey was four, he was spending quite a few hours a day watching math and science DVDs, clicking through it all by himself, and as a result he learned how to read and do math quite early.

Advance the clock. Now he is nine, and wild about videos, but not the educational "Baby Einstein" variety. He is hooked on digital video games and his mom is quite concerned. The video games are taking over all his time and displacing other interests. Trey's mom started narrowing Trey's video interactions after realizing that he didn't want to sign up for any after-school activities that might cut into his game time. Fortunately, Trey's mom woke up to their dilemma and quickly took steps to limit his on-screen time.

A report by the USC Center for the Digital Future Survey revealed a troubling downside to our children's technology use. The report revealed that parents are beginning to see that the family's plugged-in time is reducing face-to-face interaction and cutting into quality family time. Dr. Michele Borba, an internationally recognized expert and author on bullying and moral development, states:

> What's potentially at stake for our plugged-in children's lives is serious, including the diminishment of the strength of our bond with our sons and daughters, the loss of strong family relationships, rituals, memories, and interactions, and stunted development of our children's empathy and social skills.[1]

We agree, to a point, that the digital world can enhance our children's cognitive growth by watching computer-generated training tools. But children also need real-life encounters to become whole persons. They need to learn communication skills, emotional intelligence, empathy, how to listen, and how to show respect to others. For example, it's not enough for them to observe the countryside or nature at work through the lens of a computer screen. Experts now call this "nature deficit disorder." Our children need to experience the countryside with its smells and sounds. And for it to be real and meaningful, children must experience nature, face-to-face and touch-to-touch!

An important point that we need to share with parents is this: if you want to protect your children from developing an addiction to the computer, Internet, smartphone, or other digital device, you need to have a very clear plan of action.

Parents' Fears about the Digital World

In speaking with parents about this issue, many feel fearful about where the digital world is taking their children. So what is it that parents fear?

- *Age-appropriate content*—at what age should children be allowed different levels of engagement?
- *Physical inactivity*—to what extent is the lack of physical activity likely to cause obesity?
- *Addiction*—where are children at greatest risk for developing an addiction?
- *Screen time*—how much screen time is acceptable for different age groups?
- *Unbalanced life*—to what extent does the over-engagement of the digital world unbalance a child's life?
- *Socialization*—Does social media exposure create a lack of social skills?
- *Education*—Does digital engagement affect learning and grades?

According to a committee of the American Academy of Pediatrics, the number one fear parents expressed about parenting in this digital age was on setting limits for their child's screen times. The recommended screen time limits for children from 0 to 19 from the American Academy of Pediatrics are shown below. It may seem a little strange to be including babies in a list like this, but keep in mind that computer tablets (like iPads) are already available for babies to pound their fists on. They are being exposed to computers long before they can even walk!

Recommended Screen Limits for Children

Children ages 0 to 2—No screen time. Babies need all five senses to develop at this stage, and the digital screen only develops two of these senses, namely seeing and hearing.

Children ages 3 to 5—One hour per day. This is the age of make-believe. They have no logic at this age so they need to spend playtime with other children.

Children ages 6 to 12—No more than ninety minutes per day.
Teenagers 13 to 19—Two hours a day.[2]

Most families are already exceeding the recommended screen time limits for children and teenagers. Only about three in ten young people say they have family rules about how much time they can spend watching television or playing video games. Even when parents do set limits, their children still spend nearly three hours a day on their computers, and this exceeds the recommended limits.[3] Most eight- to eighteen-year-olds spend seven to eight hours a day looking at their screens, so we can see why parents need to be concerned about their family's digital usage.

The implementation of the "digital protection plan" that we propose will not only have the benefit of decreasing your child's risk of developing an Internet addiction but, in turn, other digital addictions as well.

To help parents manage their children's digital usage, we present the following seven-step plan of action. It is easily implemented and can be incorporated into your family's lifestyle in a very short period of time.

Step 1: Lay a Foundation of Trust

One essential ingredient in any plan that attempts to limit children's involvement in their digital life is the building of trust between parents and children. While effective parenting in general requires a foundation of trust, attempting to limit or manage digital activity is even more demanding of trust. The reason is that other parents are not going to be good role models. Many do not see any risk in the digital world at all or are not aware of the need to implement digital boundaries. When your children see friends or neighbors' kids romping freely around the digital world while they are being limited, they are not going to be happy campers. You will need to build as much trust with your children as you can to overcome their resistance.

Key components for building trust:

- Parents build trust by showing unconditional love and affection. Praise your children whenever they do the right thing, and when they do not, gently draw their attention to what went wrong and encourage them to try again.

- Keep in mind that children want, need, and expect parents to set clear limits. Consistency will always build trust. When a child knows that a certain behavior will not be tolerated, that child will slowly come to accept your wishes. When you always praise the right behavior, that behavior becomes cemented into a child's life.

- Finally, parents who are good listeners build stronger trust than those who are not. So allow your child to explain why they broke the rules. Children will be more compliant when they fully understand and know where parents are coming from, and communicating needs to be age appropriate. You do not spend time responding to the repeated "why's" from a three-year-old. You respond simply with a "Because I say so!" At age six, a child begins to need sensible and reasonable explanations and information.

Step 2: Stay Informed about the Digital World

For the sake of their children, parents owe it to them to stay digitally up-to-date. The nature of the digital world is rapidly changing. When the Internet first arrived, it offered mostly benign information and communication. Its evolution has been so rapid and the opportunities for misuse are now so rampant that most parents, and adults in general, find it difficult to keep abreast of the consequences of these changes.

Fortunately, a lot of attention is now being given to "cyber bandits," online crime, security risks, identification thefts, and online bullying and sexual abuse. The state of New York introduced an Internet Crimes Against Children Task Force and has found numerous instances of online criminal activity involving adults who use the Internet to victimize young people and children. One threat often overlooked by parents is the dissemination of indecent sexual materials to minors over the Internet, making it now the medium of choice for pedophiles!

To protect children from such online predators, parents must be proactive and stay up-to-date about what is going on in the digital world.

Ways Parents Can Stay Informed

- Access the Internet itself and see what is being reported there. It is a rich source of information. For example, CNN.com has subsections on technology and health that regularly report news pertaining to Internet abuse and risks to children.

- Regularly do a Google search for "Internet risk for children" and download any relevant information that might be helpful to you and your family.
- Keep a lookout for news and programs on television that might be informative. PBS frequently offers programs that look at new developments in science and social life.

Step 3: Love Enough to Set Limits on Using Digital Devices

Never in human history have children been exposed to such a high degree of freedom and high level of stimulation. As Dennis Prager, sociologist and well-known syndicated radio host, says:

> Today's young people have the ability to experience excitement more than any generation in history. Outside of school, excitement is available almost 24/7. MTV is exciting (MTV has done far more damage to this generation than has the tobacco industry); video games are exciting; the nearly all-pervasive sexual stimuli are exciting; MySpace (largely a human cesspool) is exciting; getting tattooed is exciting; piercings are exciting; many pictures and videos on the Internet are exciting. The list of exciting things many children experience is as long as there are hours in the day. However, all this excitement is actually inhibiting our children's ability to enjoy life and therefore be happy. All this excitement renders young people jaded, not happy.[4]

More importantly, parts of our digital culture target children intentionally, especially teenagers and young adults. For many children of busy or stressed-out parents, the exposure to the digital world is accompanied with the frightening freedom young people have to do more or less as they please.

It is no surprise that when parents set boundaries, not just for technology usage, but also in other areas of a child's life, there will be pushback. Resistance comes with the territory and is to be expected. The child who never hears the word "no" from a parent is most likely to become an unhappy, stressed-out child. One of the wisest of persons that I (Dr. Hart) have ever encountered is Erma Bombeck. I suppose that not too many of our younger readers will recognize the name, sadly! She was a humorist who achieved great popularity for her newspaper columns that described suburban home life from the mid-1960s until the late 1990s. She published fifteen books, most of them bestsellers.

In one of her newspaper columns, she describes how being a mom was one of the hardest, yet most rewarding jobs on the face of the earth, and how she responded to a common expression from a child who tried to get his or her own way with the familiar, "You don't love me!" She writes: "Someday, when my children are old enough to understand the logic that motivates a mother, I'll tell them . . . 'I loved you enough to bug you about where you were going, with whom and what time you would get home.'"[5] Then she ends her long list of the things she would want to tell them with these touching words:

> But most of all, I loved you enough to say "no" when you hated me for it, and that was the hardest part of all.[6]

Erma Bombeck is right on target here. "No" is not the ugliest of words a parent must use, but sometimes the most loving. Your no's give meaning to your yeses. Effective planning and boundary setting in today's digital world communicates caring. It says, "I cannot allow you to get into trouble. I love you too much for that. I want you to be the best person you can possibly be. So you have to trust me; my judgment is better than yours and my love for you demands that I say no when I must. Yes, you probably don't understand and almost certainly want to shout out 'you don't love me,' but one day you will be a parent yourself and will understand."

Children will not always see it this way. How can they? They are too immature to understand, but the day will come when they will appreciate it, especially when they become parents! So, say no appropriately, consistently, and lovingly, and your children will one day bless you for it.

Children will often respond with overstatements in attempting to defend what they want to do. The classic overstatement is "Everyone is doing it." It is universal. I've heard kids say it in South Africa, Australia, and just about every country I've visited. Parents must stick to their guns and not give in to these distractions. Deep down children do not want spineless parents. It's sad, but your advice won't be appreciated until they are adults, and possibly parents, themselves.

Step 4: Protecting Your Children's Social Skills

There is no doubt that developing effective social skills is essential for our children to thrive. These skills are important in building relationships, building strong marriages, and being successful at your work.

There are very few jobs or careers where you can isolate yourself and never encounter work colleagues. It's hard to underestimate the impact that good social skills have on your career, but they are essential. In fact, across the board and in a wide variety of businesses, people would rather work with someone who is incompetent but likable than with someone who is skilled but obnoxious.

But what has this got to do with our digital world? As we have tried to show earlier, our digital social media has become a major component of our lives. We have become complacent and probably oblivious to its hazardous consequences. The way we now socialize in the digital age is serious business and now starts very early in a child's life. While this can offer some helpful social training, it can also lead to a host of problems such as depression, changing sleep and eating habits, experiencing mood swings, hanging out with different friends, or becoming socially isolated. The good news is that we can shape our children's behaviors so they can become socially healthier. What can parents do?

Strategies for Building Social Skills

1. The *first strategy* is for parents to ensure that they never give up THEIR responsibility for shaping their children's social skills, from the earliest ages on up. If your very young child has a "baby" computer with all its digital toys, make sure you limit the amount of time he or she plays with them. Also, ensure that you have more social contact with your child than they have with their digital gadget. Never let the screens dominate or be a substitute for your physical contacts. Children need to experience real physical touches, hear real voices, and see real people's faces much more than digital ones. Be the primary socializing tool for your children, and it will help prevent later addictions to social media. Remember real love will prevail. Also, most children don't mean to be irresponsible here but often engage in social media activities at inappropriate times because their friends are doing it. Children are not mature enough to realize that sleep deprivation can have severe consequences for learning as well as for their physical and mental health.

2. The *second strategy* is to not allow your children's contacts with friends over computers or digital applications to become a substitute for REAL friendships. Try to hold to the minimum age guideline of thirteen before you let your child sign up for

Facebook—even though currently Facebook is trying to remove the age restriction. Why is this important? Because some scientists are now convinced that our emotional attachments and empathy building to others is better formed in face-to-face encounters than on a computer screen. As one expert puts it: "Tech savvy our children are; life savvy they are not."[7] Children who socialize mainly via social media do not grasp the finer points of social interaction; they need human contact, coaching, and modeling.

With children and young teenagers, know every form of social media they might be using. Ensure they are not socializing with total strangers, as pedophiles can masquerade as children on the Internet. Your children should only communicate over the Internet with real friends that they see personally and frequently, such as schoolmates or friends from church. While it is possible that a child could become an online friend with someone, say, in Timbuktu, the risks associated with becoming too closely bonded with total strangers are high. You have no idea if they are really in Timbuktu or not, or if they are misleading your child.

3. The *third strategy* is to encourage your children to always build REAL friendships, not just social media friendships. In other words, while social media can be an effective tool for augmenting real friendships, it is not best to build a wider span of friendships with total strangers. Try to prevent extreme texting with their friends. Although the occasional texting between friends can be beneficial, the risk of it becoming extreme, and therefore addicting, is very high. Reports show that teens often text thousands of times each month. In one case, a report showed a teen that had texted 14,000 times in one month. Texting can also be risky, as kids sometimes use texting for flirting, sexual play, bullying, and talking about drugs or alcohol. Often the worst of a teen comes out when texting. Try to monitor your child's texting without being too invasive in older teens. Talking regularly with your children and building a strong, open relationship is always the best protection.

4. The *fourth strategy* is to not tolerate any sexting. It is clearly a major distorter of sexuality, enhances impulsivity, and can foster serious sexual misbehavior. The underlying issue is the importance of healthy sexual instruction and dialogue between parents and children.

Step 5: Set Up a Digital Contract

Setting up a digital contract or "pledge" can help a parent protect children from abusing their Internet privileges. Creating a pledge or contract for yourself can also improve your own control.

There are three components to a digital contract. First, and easiest, is that it must spell out the time limits of digital usage. Second, there needs to be some form of reinforcement for complying with the contract, so that the child feels it is a worthwhile endeavor. In the mental health field we call this "contingency management," and it is widely used in shaping children's and adults' behavior. Third, parents have to be prepared to implement the clear and reasonable consequences agreed on for violations of the plan. Dealing with the violations of the contract is the most challenging part for the parent. It is easy to turn away or ignore the noncompliance, or to overreact, become angry, and punish the child. Either response is not helpful.

Preparing a Digital Contract

In appendices B and C, we offer sample contracts that you can use to model your own family's contracts. The important thing is to have clearly defined boundaries, adjusted appropriately to the age of your children. Consequences for breaking the contract should be laid out between parents and children beforehand. Have some age-appropriate discussions with your children before you present them with a final contract. If done together in love, it can be a way for a family to bond in the quest for a united, healthy use of the digital world. Some families print and post their contract on or near the family computer.

Rewarding Digital Contract Compliance

The best reward for reinforcing desired behaviors in children is by praising them when they comply. Praise is the most powerful rewarder of behavior. These are some basic, easy-to-implement principles that parents can utilize in reinforcing their digital contract.

- *Token system*: This is a reward system where a child can earn a token for a single act of compliance or completing a task. The tokens are accumulated and then "cashed in" for a gift or privilege. If the contract says that all computers must be turned off

at 9:00 p.m. or before going to bed, then every time the child does this, one of the parents can give the token with lots of appreciation and praise.
Sometimes buttons or other small objects serve as tokens. Money can also be used as the token. It is better not to use money as the immediate reward, because you may not always have the right amount for the intended gift. It is preferable to give money only as the final reward when the child has accumulated a certain number of tokens. Visits to special places can also serve as a reward. For instance, if you know that your child desperately wants to go to Disneyland or see a particular movie, you can easily set up the value of the token by specifying how many times a child should comply in order to earn the visit.

- *Voucher system*: The use of vouchers, rather than tokens, can sometimes be more effective in older teenagers where collecting buttons or other representative objects is seen as childish. The same basic principle as the token system is applied, except that the teenager earns a voucher that accumulates until you reach the number of vouchers needed to earn whatever you have agreed on. You don't have to have a specified activity or object in mind at the time they are collected. Often they can be "traded" for a special privilege. For example, if a teenage daughter is pleading to pay a visit to a friend who has moved to another part of the country, a voucher system could be set up for the teenager to earn that trip.

Try to guard against overreacting whenever a child misses gaining a token or voucher. Getting angry, displaying frustration, or punishing a child works against these reward systems. Treat it in a matter-of-fact way, and when a token is earned, do not give it without praise. A contract is a contract, so be consistent in implementing it.

Dealing with Noncompliance of the Digital Contract

There will come a time, even in the best of families, when a child will blunder and a major breach of the contract will occur. How you deal with these breaches is extremely important, but dealing with them is a must.
The main reason why family rules are not followed is if there are no clear consequences for violating them. Even when there are

consequences spelled out, parents may be inconsistent in enforcing them.

The best consequences (we prefer not to see them as forms of punishment) are those that can be implemented immediately and are appropriate in severity to the misbehavior. Let us make one very important point: In behavioral therapy, there is a big difference between "discipline" (where the goal is to change or improve behavior) and "punishment" (where the goal is to punish without regard to whether or not the behavior changes). You can consult my (Dr. Hart's) book *Stress and Your Child* for more information about how to achieve maximum and effective change in children's behavior, especially when it is more serious.[8]

In less serious cases, you can do the following. Let's assume that you have a rule that your twelve-year-old son Billy must not do any texting after 10:00 p.m. or after going to bed. A consequence for violating this rule cannot be "Billy, you will not get a new cell phone next year." Why is this not appropriate? First, the consequence is too delayed from the current violation and is not likely to have any lasting effect. Second, the consequence is too severe. Billy will just give up participating in the agreement.

It is best to have a consequence that has an immediate effect, and that is seen as fair. This way Billy won't just give up hope and look for a way he can hide his behavior. For instance, if the consequence is that Billy will have to surrender his cell phone for the rest of the evening, and if he disobeys again, it will be taken away for two evenings, Billy will quickly realize that it is in his best interest to follow the agreed-upon rules. If parents incrementally enforce the consequence with fairness and consistency every time the rule is violated, not just occasionally, the discipline will be more effective.

BEST NONCOMPLIANCE CONSEQUENCES

The best discipline consequences for not complying with an agreed behavior are those that

- Can be immediately and consistently implemented every time there is misbehavior.
- Will cause your child some disappointment because they really do not want to lose whatever their privilege is.

• Are not so punitive as to feel it is unfair or so severe and hurtful that the child loses all interest in collaborating.

Step 6: Keep the Internet Safe

One of the most commonly overlooked ways for protecting kids on the Internet is to have complete control over how you get access to it. Most homes have a cable or satellite system connected to a router that delivers the Internet to members of the family either through a wire or wirelessly.

Parents must remember that our children are more technologically savvy than we are. So, if you try to restrict or block some aspect of their access to the web, they will know, or will quickly find out, how to circumvent even the most powerful blocking or limiting software. Kids share this information with each other all the time. They know how to reset a router and circumvent any firewalls in both the router and the computer. Also, remember that your Internet supplier does not guarantee Internet safety. It is entirely up to you to safeguard your family's access to the Internet. This means that *you* have to be the one who decides the extent and degree of freedom your child has when accessing the Internet, and using other digital access gadgets as well.

Here are some tips to keep in mind:

INTERNET ACCESS SAFETY TIPS

• Ensure that your child does not have direct access to your router. A simple press of the reset button can cancel any protection that may have been set up. Once reset, most routers default to the factory settings and provide wide-open wireless access with no encryption or protection of your personal information. You can use a service called OpenDNS Family Shield and each device in your home sharing your Internet connection gets protected.

• Set router-enforced time limits for Internet access by implementing a setting that turns it off at a certain time of the day. This will disconnect both the cable and wireless access. The time you set to turn off your router will depend on the age of your children. Older teens may need to have access to the Internet at times similar to yours, but younger children may have to turn off their computers at an earlier time. Not all routers have this option, but it is an option you can look for.

- Scan for wireless access points close to your home. A neighbor, for instance, may have a wide-open Internet wireless access point, so when your Internet is off, a smart child can still go online with the neighbor's wireless Internet connection, all in the privacy of his or her bedroom. I (Dr. Hart) have several neighbors who have open wireless connections. On one occasion, I actually "borrowed" a neighbor's Internet connection when my server was down. If I can do it, your child can also!

- Gaming systems and mobile devices should have Parental Control features installed and checked regularly that they are working. Get to know what control features your child's devices have in place and ensure that they are working.

    Parental control software to consider:
    - BSecure Online—The most endorsed and trusted provider of parental controls software for the family.
    - iWonderPro—The ultimate parental control web browser with controls exceeding anything available today! Utilizing advanced GPS technology, you can see exactly where your kids are when they surf the web, and adult sites are blocked automatically.
    - Safe Eyes—Mac, PC, and iOS compatible software that protects your family from harmful content and other dangers on the Internet.
    - Net Nanny—A powerful, yet simple to use parental control and Internet safety solution that helps parents protect their children and monitor their Internet use. Filter website content, monitor Facebook, set time controls, block inappropriate games, and much more.
    - Webwatcher—Totally invisible, records all popular computer/Internet activity such as all chat, email activity, IM's, Facebook/MySpace activity, and more. Plus you can access all recorded logs from any computer.

- Keep all computers in an open area where all technology activity can be observed.

- Since most children know how to erase their Internet tracks by deleting browser histories, consider installing a logging device in your router or other monitoring software that can track all Internet activity. These Internet tools should be able to keep your children safe and far removed from undesirable websites.

Step 7: Stay Involved in Your Children's Digital Lives

The most effective protection a parent can offer a child is to be intimately involved in their lives, both inside and outside the home. There is so much risk attached to using the Internet that no parent should allow his or her children to enter that world unsupervised. You would not turn them loose in a gang-infested ghetto, so why would you let them enter the digital universe without supervision?

One of the gravest consequences of our digital technology is that it has widened the communication gap between parents and children and has increased the independence of the child from the parent. Several studies have shown that parents do not know what is going on in the lives of their children, because of the communication gap and the lack of contact with their children.

Set aside some time every week to get an update from your child about what is happening in their world, and ask how they feel about the role their Internet connections are playing in their lives. Establishing a regular time for conversation can help promote transparency.

Many parents report that because they did not establish regular conversations with their children in earlier years, any attempt at conversation with their children about their Internet usage is not easy. So, the earlier you start and continue these conversations through their teenage years the better. Let them talk while you listen, giving them your full attention. Yes, this means turning off your computer as well! Do not lecture or express disappointment, just listen and show empathy, and offer suggestions if asked.

The Stealth American Plague

Trace Embry, the founder and executive director of Shepherd's Hill Academy (SHA), a Christ-centered and biblically based residential program and school that serves families of troubled teenagers between the ages of twelve and seventeen, shared what he is observing at his center.[9]

I (Trace) have noticed an incredible difference in the behavior, attitude, and overall mental, emotional, and spiritual health of newly enrolled students over the past decade especially in the last few years. Being born into the digital world, this new generation of young people seems to be hardwired, like robots, with insatiable appetites for things that are killing them from the inside out.

When kids come to our program for a year, SHA kids have virtually no access to television, iPods, cell phones, video games, movies, bombastic music, inappropriate entertainment, computers, or any other technological devices requiring screens, keyboards, or electricity. They are reduced to the basics of life. Over the years, we've discovered that when kids first come, their ability to reason, contemplate, and problem solve just isn't there, at least not as it should be for their age group. Many come with little ability to think abstractly or objectively. Most are very narcissistic and lack empathy, while some appear to have no conscience whatsoever. But again, over time their critical, creative, and constructive thinking capacities begin to return to them as they engage in activities, such as construction projects, preparing meals, and other problem-solving tasks that require those parts of the brain to fire again.

Taking away virtually all technological stimuli, however, without filling the void with healthy, loving relationships and other healthy activities can result in a less-than-successful endeavor. Without teaching them the science behind the brain damage due to digital gluttony, training them in God's Word, training them in Christian apologetics, exercising discipline and accountability, allowing time for contemplative thought and prayer, challenging them with difficult and thought-provoking tasks, and encouraging them to serve others, boredom and disillusionment can quickly return and overtake them.

That's when cravings return for the same dumbing-down stimuli they routinely see their peers and the masses using. Some of the kids we see couldn't do homework, or go from point A to point B, without wearing headphones to keep them amused. Some couldn't focus long enough to do homework at all because it just wasn't stimulating enough. Bible reading or Bible study would have been considered exercises in mental brutality! Once their ability to contemplate returns to them, their prayer life begins, and so does their healing.

We see many parents using digital stimuli as babysitters and pacifiers for not just their young children but their teens as well. But these "babysitters" and "pacifiers" are too often abusing and poisoning our kids all the while. Parents often falsely assume that, because their teens aren't running in the streets and hanging out in the "seedy side of town," all is well. However, as their teens spend hour upon hour stowed away in the perceived safety of their own private digital arcades (also known as bedrooms), the "seedy side of town" is being explored and engaged virtually unnoticed!

When parents allow these techno marathons night after night, it sends a message to their children. It actually conjures up fear, insecurity, and disrespect for their parents. This is magnified when parents are preoccupied and caught up in their own techno worlds, whether it is television or something else. My experience has convinced me that, deep inside, kids really want their parents to put limits, not just on their techno use, but many other areas of their lives also. Firm boundaries, high standards, and good examples, are, believe it or not, what brings kids the security and significance they are so desperate for today. It's essential for their healing. Without it, kids are likely to find security and significance in all the wrong people, places, and things.

Digital technology can't offer kids what they are craving deep down in their souls. They want real adults, with real answers and real feelings and emotions. They want someone to love and respect. A machine or a computerized device can't love or appreciate anyone; neither can it receive love, respect, or appreciation.

What We Can Do about It

Trace Embry offers us valuable wisdom from his frontline work with troubled digital natives. His program of healing is outstanding and desperately needs to be followed by others seeking to treat teenage problems. We encourage you to make it a priority to be a "plugged-in" parent—a parent who stays abreast of what is happening in the digital world. Let your children know that you are interested in how they use the digital world because it's in their best interest and you love them. The most powerful source of impact on shaping a child is the strength of their relationship with their parents. There is no computer program or shortcut for this. It's achieved by clear, face-to-face communication with your children in a loving and caring way. What your child really wants is your love, your time, and your presence. They want you.

For parents of young kids and for teenagers who have already acquired unhealthy appetites for digital stimuli, below are a few tips to limit your child's chances of acquiring a debilitating digital addiction.

TEN TOUGH TECHNOLOGY TIPS

1. *Be alert.* Watch, listen, learn, and engage with your kids. When your kids are playing video games, watching television, or engaging in some other digital activity, use these times as teachable moments. Come to grips with the fact that neither you nor your kids are immune to technology's ability to entice and are not above abusing yourselves or someone else with technology. Don't assume your kids are always going to make the right choices when using technology.

2. *Create a safe home environment* that makes it easy for your kids to share their hearts' desires, concerns, apprehensions, fears, temptations, and experiences in all areas of their technological experience, even their mistakes. They must know it's safe to discuss these things with you, and do it regularly.

3. *Establish good media habits.* Lead the way. Change your attitude to align with Christ's attitude toward media in your home, and then model it before your kids. Kids are much more likely to acquire appetites for what they are often being exposed to. Media should be a privilege instead of a constant activity that is simply taken for granted. Have your kids get into the habit of asking permission to use anything with a screen or keyboard, while in your house. Consider a ban on headphones in your home.

4. *Attach all media to a system of accountability.* Location is everything. Keep it in a common area. Never allow a computer or a television in your child's room. Have filters for everything. Know all their passwords and codes. Snoop often, and check history often. Do your best to make media use a family affair. Consider media and digital fasts as a family. Consider having a time when all technology is checked in and locked up each night. Have each sibling monitor and hold one another accountable. Allow an outside objective source to review and critique your family's media habits. This could be a pastor, family member, or trusted friend.

5. *Determine a media diet and stick to it.* Only you will know that balance. Allow your kids to help make it. They will often

be stricter on themselves than you will be on them. Allow your kids a cell phone that is nothing more than a phone. Limit leaving your kids alone. When you must, have a system that locks everything but their phone.

6. *Recognize the warning signs.* Is your child tired in the morning because he's up all night? Has he lost his appetite for things he normally loves? Is he withdrawn from the family? Is he irritable, defensive, and touchy when asked about his computer habits? Does the screen on the computer seem to suddenly change often as you walk by him? Remember, you could be a foot away and never know what he's viewing.

7. *Encourage media literacy and accountability in your church, in your social club, and with your friends.* This fosters the authoritative community that encourages accountability and standards that transcend your home, making your community a more trustworthy environment.

8. *Be proactive in encouraging good wholesome media habits.* There are many websites like www.pluggedin.com and others that can help families navigate the sea of entertainment alternatives. Instead of telling our kids what they can't be exposed to, give them a number of healthy options in which they can engage. This will train their appetites for more wholesome entertainment.

9. *Give them alternative entertainment activities.* Digital entertainment isn't the only option. Sports, hobbies, board games, and books are just a few of the myriad of nondigital activities that kids can rebuild and refresh their minds and bodies with. Steer them toward balance in their lives.

10. TURN IT OFF!

Discussion Questions

1. Discuss your experience with "Baby Einstein" or any other digital technology toy for children.

2. How would you like to stay informed about the digital world's effects on families?

3. Which key components of trust between you and your child, as discussed in this chapter, do you need to work on?

4. What do you think about Erma Bombeck's statement, "I loved you enough to say 'no'"? How has it challenged you as a parent?

5. Has the digital world had any effect on your child's socializing skills? Explain.

6. If you intend to use them, discuss how you are going to implement the digital contracts we offer.

10

Protecting Your "Godspace"

Are you tired? Worn out? Burned out on religion? Come
  to me.
Get away with me and you'll recover your life. I'll show
  you how to take a real rest.
Walk with me and work with me—watch how I do it.
Learn the unforced rhythms of grace.
I won't lay anything heavy or ill-fitting on you.
Keep company with me and you'll learn to live freely
  and lightly.

Matthew 11:28–30 Message

Our final chapter is an invitation for you to "untether," come away, and recover your real life in Christ. We want to ask you: Are you tired? Worn out? Burned out from life in the digital world? Does living freely and lightly sound too good to be true? Are you tethered to your "always-on" technology and the people who can always reach you?

Perhaps the most profound lesson we have learned in researching and writing this book is how many of us are tired, worn out, and burned out. We have seen firsthand how easy it is to waste time doing trivial stuff on the Internet, while neglecting those things that really matter in our lives. Jesus' call in the Scripture, cited above, to come and keep company with him seems faint with all the noise in our present world. We need to be aware of how easy it is to neglect creating time and space for God—a Godspace—amidst all the demands on our attention. If we don't, we could wake up one day and discover that there is no space left in our lives for God. We define *Godspace* as a sacred space where we disconnect from our technology and meet God without distractions. The digital invasion has made us deprive ourselves of every opportunity for disconnection. Our constant connection and stimulation is not a modern problem—man has always desired constant connection; it's just never been possible until now. In closing our book, we share with you a "Biblical Theology of Technology," to help protect your Godspace.

There is a growing concern that the Internet is causing many people to lose their faith. Apologist Josh McDowell shares this view; "Atheists and skeptics now have equal access to our children just as your youth pastor and you have, which is why the number of Christian youth who believe in the fundamentals of Christianity is decreasing."[1] With the abundance of knowledge and information now flooding our children, they can easily become distracted, disillusioned, and skeptical in their relationship with God. As parents we must also do all we can to protect our children's Godspace as well as our own.

Throughout this book, our focus has been on how we are becoming more and more dependent on our digital technology, and less reliant on God. This is not just our experience. Scores of Christian believers we have spoken to report the same struggle. "We are running out of time in our daily life, and there is very little left of it to give to God," is what many are saying today.

It's almost as if the distractions that we allow the digital world to impose on us is a form of an idol that we worship instead of God. Timothy Keller, in his book *Counterfeit Gods*, expresses it this way: "Idols are anything that become more important to us than God; anything that can absorb our heart and imagination more than God, and that seek to give us what God alone can give."[2] This is an apt definition of how our modern digital technology can easily become idolatrous.

If, as Keller suggests, an idol is anything that is so important to you that if you were to lose it, you would feel that life wasn't worth living, then could we become guilty of creating "counterfeit Gods"? The psalmist penned similar words about idols: "But their idols are silver and gold, made by human hands. They have mouths, but cannot speak, eyes, but cannot see. They have ears, but cannot hear, noses, but cannot smell. They have hands, but cannot feel, feet, but cannot walk, nor can they utter a sound with their throats. Those who make them will be like them, and so will all who trust in them" (Ps. 115:4–8). Yes, the psalmist is referring to idols of silver and gold, so how can we possibly compare them with the digital world? What we want to stress is that whatever crowds out our space for God has the potential to become an idol in the biblical sense of the word.

Freeing Up Space for God

People in a hurry rob themselves of recovery time. It can be stress, an addiction, or simply fatigue that is the thief, and today many are showing signs of physiological disintegration. The pace of life is too fast and there is not enough rest for the body to recuperate. Our minds have little time to meditate and pray, so problems are never resolved or put into perspective. We see Christians today living off other people's spiritual experiences, many through blogs, with nothing of their own to show for it. Many are scattered, distracted, and un-centered, settling for a "one-inch deep" spirituality, rather than an abundant life. While we cannot blame all spiritual struggles on our overuse of digital technology, it plays a major role in robbing us of our Godspace.

The digital world, wonderful as it might appear, demands time from all of us. It is a time guzzler, because it is so powerful in relieving boredom. It speeds up the way we do things and gives us an adrenaline rush but can easily absorb the free time needed for our Godspace.

Facebook, Twitter, MySpace, YouTube, LinkedIn, Flickr, Pinterest, texting, or just plain emails are "time ravenous." While speaking with Christians, we keep hearing one consistent message: "I'm finding it more and more difficult to find time for God." Pastors and church members, male and female, young and old, are all being impacted, if you want a spiritual life, you will have to make space for it. It won't come naturally.

See Your Godspace as Sacred

The first step toward protecting your Godspace is to see the time you spend with God as sacred. For a space to be sacred, it needs to be interruption free. Making space for God will also require discipline. You might get it right one week, and then the next, find that the digital invasion slips in unnoticed and robs you of space. But we have to create space and time free of all other demands if we want to experience God.

The digital world has robbed our Godspace in another important way. It has made us informationally rich, but as a consequence, spiritually poor. It isn't information that fosters our Godspace, but, paradoxically, the absence of information. Isn't that what the Scripture "Be still, and know that I am God" (Ps. 46:10) really means? Interestingly, the word translated "be still" comes from the Hebrew term *raphah* and means "to be weak, to let go, to release and surrender." We have to "be still," so that we can know that he is God. It is a call to surrender, do nothing, and engage your spiritual serenity. This can only be achieved when we disengage from our digital world.

Furthermore, our lack of Godspace is not only a problem with individuals, but applies to churches as well. Author and blogger Tim Challies explains it this way: "If we are a distracted people and a distracted society, it stands to reason that we would also be a distracted church, a church with a diminished ability to think deeply, to cultivate concentration, to emphasize slow, deliberate thoughtful meditation."[3] Most Christians have been taught that prayer and devotional time should be the first activity of their day. In reality, for most of us, it is to check our email. For others it is voice mail, text messages, tweets, and the latest Facebook notifications.

Cultivating the Place

Technology is not very good at helping us create space in time and activity, and space is becoming our scarcest commodity. Fire burns because of the space we leave between the logs—breathing space, if you will. Our life must also have space in order to "breathe." Think about the last time you unplugged and claimed some space in your time, and just sat still for a while in complete silence. You may find it helpful if you keep a log of these times, if only to see how seldom you do it.

The realization of how seldom I've really unplugged at a deep level came for me (Dr. Hart) just a couple of months ago. It was quite a revelation. It took the worst windstorm that has ever struck the Los

Angeles area to shake me up and help me regain an appreciation for simple stillness and quietness. The windstorm struck shortly after dark. The wind howled all through the night. I could hear trees being uprooted outside. All my wife and I, as well as our little dog, Andy, could do was lie in our beds and "ride it out."

But that night was to be the least of my trouble. Fallen trees and flying debris devastated the whole neighborhood, and all our electric power was gone. It meant no television, smartphone, or Internet access. It didn't take long for me to realize how hooked I had become on my digital gadgets. The first day wasn't too bad. My smartphone and laptop were fully charged. I prayed that the electricity would return before dark. It didn't. By the second day, all the batteries were dead, so I had no external communication whatsoever. My daughters were out of town, so there was no digital device I could even borrow from them.

I was very antsy that second night and realized I was experiencing some withdrawal symptoms. After a while, I began to feel at ease, even relieved, that I didn't have to retrieve any emails or bother about any messages. But I kept feeling that something was missing. And it was—the Internet, of course. There was no form of entertainment. I tried to do some cleaning up outside. By the next evening, I was really troubled again. It felt like something BIG was missing. There was nothing to do but just sit around and talk with my wife. As a clinician, I have seen many alcoholics in recovery over the years, but never really felt like an addict about my computer and the Internet. Perhaps it was not as bad as what real addicts experience, but I sure felt something was missing.

As the week went by, my wife and I found ourselves spending more time in prayer, having deep conversations, and experiencing a clear sense of connection with God, something I haven't really felt for a long time. There was never much "space" for it. When power was finally restored a week later, I almost felt a sense of disappointment. I was just beginning to re-create some real Godspace in my life, and I didn't want to give it up.

The important lesson I learned from this experience was how dependent and distracted I had become in my use of the digital world. Not that I should or would shut down all Internet engagement, but I was reminded that I needed to be intentional about taking "time off" from my many digital engagements if I was going to preserve some space in my life for God.

So, why do we neglect this sacred space so easily? Partly it is because spending time in silence can be uncomfortable when you are accustomed to being perpetually on the go. We are more apt to soothe our fears and desires by being connected to the Internet than by getting alone and spending some time with God.

We are also aware that many of us, particularly digital natives, don't really know what our Godspace should look like. So let us identify the more important characteristics that can make up our Godspace. Of course, we may differ in our individual preferences; so while you review the list below, consider what might be the essentials for your Godspace:

YOUR GODSPACE

- *A place where you feel safe.* We can come to God just as we are and be seen, valued, and heard, fearing nothing. Be simple in your desires and expectations because God comes to us in simple ways.

- *An intimate place.* It is where you and God meet—just the two of you. No intruders allowed. Put a sign on your door to announce that you do not want to be disturbed.

- *An insightful place.* It is where we come to know who God really is and who we really are, while he offers us his infinite resources.

- *A communicating space.* It is here that the divine dialogue takes place. We don't just talk but also listen attentively. This is where we can share our deepest secrets and listen to the promptings of God's wisdom.

- *A sharing place.* We are not alone in this place, but are one with those we love, the members of our family, and the church. Taking space alone is not selfish. It is in this place that we join with others and share our corporate worship.

- *A quiet place.* It must be a silent place, because it is silence that re-engages our thoughts and helps us listen to God's small voice. Be patient as you attempt to quiet your mind and body.

- *A growing place.* It is where the seeds of godliness are planted, watered, and nurtured. Resist the temptation to leave this time for more "productive" work. God is at work when we are not, making us the person he wants us to become.

- *A healing place.* From heartaches to headaches, feelings of happiness to hopelessness, God is here to help us heal whatever is broken. God's healing presence can help you address the long-standing cries of your heart.

- A *heart place*. It is here that our hearts meet, we delighting in him and he delighting in us. We can pour out our hearts to him and know that he longs to give us the desires of our heart.

- A *forgiving place*. Here, all judgment is set aside as we seek his forgiveness. And his forgiveness flows abundantly in response to our confessions.

Protecting Your Godspace

> You must never face the day until you have faced God, nor look into the face of others until you have looked into his.[4]
>
> L. B. Cowman

What is encouraging about modern neuroscience research is that it is actually helping us better understand how our brain can be robbed of Godspace. Scientists tell us that they are already seeing a diminished ability to reflect, meditate, or contemplate in those who over-engage with the digital world. With these decreased abilities, our intellectual capacity is also on the decline. While this foretells serious consequences for how we learn or develop our creativity, our greatest peril is that we can also lose our ability to commune with God. If we can't disengage from our digital technology and keep a vital Godspace alive, we may not be able to engage with God at all. We will not have the physical brain mechanisms to make this connection. Moreover, just in case you think this is a little far-fetched, it would only take a neurosurgeon a minute to cut a few connections in the brain, and our ability to experience God would be gone. In other words, we need a healthy brain in order to maintain a healthy connection with God.

Dr. Gary Small, a neuroscientist and expert on Alzheimer's disease and aging, has spent a lot of time researching the effects of the digital world on our brain. He has this to report:

> Technology side effects appear to be suppressing prefrontal lobe executive skills in the brain. Today, video-game-brain, Internet addiction, and other technology side effects appear to be suppressing frontal lobe executive skills and our ability to communicate face-to-face.[5]

Our conversations with others help us to have conversations with ourselves and in turn to have conversations with God. If you can't communicate in a healthy way with people, you will also struggle to connect with God and to have good self-awareness.

Another leading neuroscientist who has researched this topic is Andrew Newberg. He explains breakthrough findings in his book *How God Changes Your Brain*.[6] It deals with how the frontal lobe in your brain creates and integrates all of your ideas about God, both positive or negative, including the logic you use to evaluate your religious and spiritual beliefs. It predicts your future relationship to God and attempts to intellectually answer all of the "why, what, and where" questions raised by spiritual issues. In essence, he states that when the prefrontal part of our brain, the part that does our main thinking, gets overloaded, it begins to shut itself down. Guess what is in our modern world that overloads the frontal part of the brain? Today's digital invasion targets mainly the frontal part of the brain, not only overusing it, but also depleting it of simple energy. This impairs our ability to think deeply, and consequently, communicate with God in a meaningful way.

This now leads to the question, How can we protect our Godspace from the digital invasion? Christian psychiatrist Dr. Curt Thompson tackles this topic in his book *Anatomy of the Soul*. He proposes that the key to this protection lies in the realm of our spiritual practices, such as regular prayer, reading Scripture, and face-to-face connections with other people who can help us develop a vital and healthy relationship with God. There is evidence that such practices can even change the way our brain uses the digital world. This is how Dr. Thompson explains it:

> Spiritual disciplines have been practiced in the lives of deeply integrated followers of God for over three thousand years. They facilitate the very things neuroscience and attachment research suggest are reflections of healthy mental states and secure attachment. Furthermore, these disciplines can strengthen the prefrontal cortex.[7]

Overcoming Spiritual Practice Prejudices

For many evangelicals, the whole notion of "spiritual practices" may be challenging, or even threatening. Some are suspicious of it, believing that it mimics Eastern religions like Transcendental Meditation or Yoga. This has led many to neglect being intentional about how they stay connected to God. Just because other religions pray doesn't mean that if we pray we are copying them. Taking time to meditate on our Scripture doesn't mean we are mimicking Eastern meditation.

For us, the phrase *spiritual practices* simply describes how we connect with God in the everyday experiences of life. It goes beyond just prayer. Why can other religions claim to experience God outside their church, while Christians see only going to church as a spiritual practice? Knowing and experiencing God should be a twenty-four-hour-a-day experience. How tragic it is if the Bible, church, and prayer have no connection to the real world. A spiritual practice or discipline is nothing more than experiencing God in the real world. It can be Bible study, prayer, going to church, or just taking time to detach from our busy life and sit alone with God.

Thankfully, there now is a growing awareness of the need for spiritual practices. In the context of our digital world invasion, this shift is very timely. It was encouraging to read an article in *Christianity Today* magazine reporting that evangelical Christians are "listening for God in ways that are different from our usual understanding of discipleship."[8] Some evangelicals are exploring more spiritual disciplines than ever before, including such practices as the value of simplicity, silence and solitude, Christian meditation, and spiritual direction. It is timely, because it is very clear that the digital world doesn't improve the quality of our spiritual life; it hampers it. Spiritual disciplines and practices are ways that can help us break out of our digital addictions and create the space for God we all need so desperately.

Exploring Spiritual Disciplines

Adele Calhoun, in her book *Spiritual Disciplines Handbook*, says, "Unplugging recognizes that a personal God creates personal beings for personal interaction."[9] Spiritual disciplines are tools that essentially help us unplug.

What are the more commonly practiced spiritual disciplines? Richard Foster, another advocate of spiritual disciplines, divides them into three groups:

1. *Inward disciplines*, which are practices in the privacy of our intimate walk with Jesus.

2. *Outward disciplines*, which affect how we interface with the world.
3. *Corporate disciplines*, which are practiced with others. Such as a group prayer meeting, or worship service.

We encourage you to explore these common spiritual practices:

fasting	godly speech	meditation
journaling	service	humility
praying the psalms	simplicity	unplugging
silence	fellowship	gratitude
solitude	breath prayers	Bible study
accountability	tithing	worship

Even Jesus modeled the practice of spiritual disciplines. He spent time in silence, solitude, and prayer. He lived a simple and sacrificial life; he studied and meditated on God's Word and ways.

In the rest of this chapter we want to focus on two of the spiritual disciplines that seem to be most lacking in our digital world, namely *silence* and *solitude*.

Silence

Silence is a "Sabbath of the mouth" and is about letting go of our inner distractions. It is probably the most challenging and least experienced spiritual discipline among Christians today. Technology is not only robbing our concentration but also our ability to just be alone and remain silent. Most of us fear or dislike being alone. When we get a chance to quiet down and shut out noise, we find that the noise from inside ourselves gets louder. It seems like the more our senses become numb to the subtle ways in which God is speaking, the greater our hunger is for sensory overload. It is ironic that what our soul longs for is silence and solitude, but instead we fill our lives with noise and activity to pack the void.

Being quiet and listening to one's soul takes time and effort. I (Dr. Frejd) have been trying for the last few years to tune in to what my soul is saying daily. I take a few minutes and sit silently, tuning in to what I am sensing and feeling, and listen to what God is saying in response. He may remind me of a Scripture or offer words of comfort or encouragement and I journal about it. Centering my heart and mind each day has become a profound experience and has given me a great sense of peace. Jesus himself said, "Peace I leave with you; my peace I give you. I do not give to you as the world gives. Do not let your hearts be troubled and do not be afraid" (John 14:27).

We cannot ignore Scripture's invitation to be still. God calls us to "lie down in green pastures" so he can "lead [us] beside quiet waters" (Ps. 23:2). Our digital world does the exact opposite, keeping us "wired" much of the time. In effect, there is a flooding of adrenaline, and then we become too tense to really connect with God and his peace. The fact is that God has built in us the need to be still. Every part of our body, and especially our brain, has a need for rest. Our brain desires and is wired for relaxation and rest from life's busyness. Amazingly, when we practice inner silence, it actually helps to restore important parts of the brain, especially the prefrontal cortex that is the thinking part of the brain, thus increasing our capacity to be creative and productive.

In the year AD 385, one of the ancient fathers known as St. Poeman forsook the world and retired into the great wilderness of Egypt. He purportedly wrote these words: "Any trial whatever that comes to you can be conquered by silence: go sit in your cell and your cell will teach you everything."[10] (A "cell" was an ancient term for a quiet, private place where one could be alone with God.)

This quote has meant a lot to me (Dr. Frejd) as I am coming out of a season of intense trials involving my husband's health and job. The time I have spent in silence, in my "cell" with God every day, has taught me much about God's love and his faithfulness. The peace I have received during my time alone and in silence with him is indescribable.

Silence, as a discipline, has many other benefits to offer also. Let us look at some of them:

THE BENEFITS OF SILENCE

- Makes room for listening to God and others.
- Gives us the freedom to observe what is really going on around us.
- Allows us time to think and reflect on our thoughts.
- Provides space to "feel" what is going on in our life.
- Lets us broaden our awareness of what is needed in our life.
- Opens us to the entry of peace.
- Invites us to know our limitations and God's vastness.

Studies have shown that the average person today, surrounded by the cyber world, can only bear about fifteen seconds of silence. Take a test for yourself. Sit down somewhere it is quiet, note the time, close your eyes, and just sit still. As soon as you feel the urge to go and do something, note the time. You might be quite surprised. Learning to remain silent and still is a habit you may have to recover. Also experiment with silence in your daily interactions with others. You may find that limiting the words you speak actually heightens your awareness of those around you and makes you less centered on yourself.

It was Mother Teresa who said, "We need silence to touch souls." Each of us needs to make the opportunity to be alone and silent, to find some space in our day to reflect, and to listen to God's voice speaking within us. Yes, it will require great effort, and our smartphone will try to disrupt our silence, so it will have to be restrained. It will feel like hard work trying to silence "the monkeys in the trees"—those thoughts that jump around in our mind. Some find it helpful to repeat a short phrase, like "You are my God" or "I belong to You," as a focus for being silent. So, every time you feel a distracting thought coming on, repeat that phrase to bring you back into focus. I (Dr. Hart) use a strategy like this all the time, including that time just before I fall asleep when my mind is most in need of silence.

The challenge to build more silent time into your life may require some sacrifice and creativity. Try taking a walk outside on your lunch hour, or drive in your car without the radio or music turned on. You can even put yourself in the closet so as not to be interrupted. If you are brave, try to go on a weekend "silent retreat" to listen to God's voice.[11] Your soul longs for silence, and God needs your silence to connect with you. It is in silence that God's voice will speak the loudest to your heart.

Solitude

Without solitude it is almost impossible to have a spiritual life.[12]

Henri Nouwen

Whereas *silence* is a "Sabbath of the mouth," *solitude* is a "Sabbath of involvement." Silence is about letting go of inner distractions and solitude is about letting go of your outer distractions.

Most of us don't spend much time alone, and even when we are physically alone, we have easy access to hundreds of friends and activities on our smartphones and tablets. Just as the digital world has robbed us of precious silence, it has also robbed us of precious solitude.

It is in solitude that we nourish our relationship with God. It's like having a bunch of friends, and there is one you want to get to know better than the others. If all the other friends are around all the time, you won't get very far. So, what do you do? You grab your friend and slip away to where you can be alone. Only then can you start to develop a real friendship.

I can remember doing this when I (Dr. Hart) first met my wife, Kathleen. When I was eighteen, the church youth group I was very active with had planned an outing with another youth group from the other side of our town, at a well-known camping area. There were quite a number of us, but one person in the other group caught my attention. There she was, looking at me. She smiled; I smiled back. My mind raced. How could I possibly get to know her with all these other young intruders around? I worked my way closer. She was still smiling, so I took the plunge, introduced myself, and asked her to go for a walk with me (I had to get her alone). She agreed, and we snuck away down to the lake where some ducks were swimming. I fell in love with her instantly, and she with me. However, without our claiming some solitude for ourselves, we would never have gotten to know each other. With too many distractions, our love affair wouldn't have happened.

While this illustration hardly deserves comparison to our relationship with God, there is some similarity. For us to get to know God, we need to sneak away and be together in solitude. Only then can God become "centered" in our lives.

We believe that God longs to be the center in our lives and for us to come to him in solitude. No words need be spoken. We can just absorb his love. The goal is to remain undistracted and wholeheartedly focus your attention on God.

Take a moment to read the poem below and let the words penetrate deep into your soul. Read it over several times until you have absorbed what it is saying, then journal whatever you feel God is revealing to your heart. You may want to write the poem on a 3x5 card so you can take it with you to work or wherever, and read it to focus your heart.

Let God Love You

Be silent.
Be still.
Alone.
Empty before your God.
Say nothing.
Ask nothing.
Be silent.
Be still.
Let your God look upon you.
That is all. God knows. God understands.
God loves you with an enormous love,
And only wants to look upon you with that love.
Quiet.
Still.
Be.
Let your God Love you.[13]

Edwina Gately

Seven Ways to Cultivate Silence and Solitude

1. Turn off the radio when you are driving.
2. Keep the television off when you're not watching it.
3. Practice listening more to others and speaking less yourself.
4. Resist the urge to text and post every experience. Hold the experience to yourself for a while.
5. Don't use your phone as an alarm clock—make a "no phones go to bed with me" rule.
6. Listen for the sounds of nature whenever you can.
7. Try to keep one ear tuned to God's voice throughout your noisy day.

Think Like Jesus—Christian Mindfulness

The urgency of slowing down, to find the time and space to think, is nothing new. Wise souls have always reminded us that the more attention we pay to the moment, the less time and energy we will need to fill it with some larger issue. In the seventeenth century the French philosopher Blaise Pascal wrote these words: "Distraction is the only thing that consoles us for our miseries, and yet it is itself the greatest of our miseries." He could just as appropriately say this about our modern age. Technology's credo is "Let me do the thinking for you." We all love the information we can obtain via digital means. Technology can't offer us the time we need to pause, reflect, and think. If anything, it robs us of this time. Furthermore, it can distract us from developing "the mind of Christ."

When engaging in the digital world, it is very easy to be distracted. The problem is that many of these distractions will leave us stressed or anxious, and eventually miserable. Pascal's comment suggests that many of our problems come from an inability to sit quietly in a room alone.[14] Digital technology shapes us through distraction, but God shapes us through our focusing on him.

As a teenager I (Dr. Hart) was deeply impacted by the novel *In His Steps* by Charles Sheldon where the popular saying "What Would Jesus Do" originated. Shortly after reading the book, I gave my life to Christ. Those words, "What would Jesus do?" were burned deep into my heart. For many months I couldn't get them out of my mind. They have followed me ever since.

Now I ask myself the question, "What would Jesus do" if he lived in our digital world? I find it difficult even to contemplate Jesus with a smartphone or sending text messages to his disciples. What is more relevant here is for us to seek the mind of God to guide us in our digital world. It's not easy knowing what Jesus would do, nor is it always easy *doing* what Jesus would do. Perhaps what is important is not just what Jesus would do but what does Jesus want ME to do with all of the technology available today. It is for this reason that we need to try to think like Jesus. There may be those who question the idea that we must be "imitators of God," but the only way we can achieve a healthy balance in our digitally invaded world is to let God shape our thinking—not just so we can deal with the challenges that face us now, but in the enormous challenges that lie ahead. This is why we need to heed Paul's challenges to "Let this mind be in you, which was also in Christ Jesus" (Phil. 2:5 KJV).

Psychology is now developing a number of therapeutic applications based on the concept of mindfulness. (Don't confuse this with what Buddhists do.) By *mindfulness*, modern psychology means "bringing one's complete attention to the present experience on a moment-to-moment basis." In short, "pay attention and stay in the present moment." Current research suggests that just "staying in the moment" therapy can be helpful in the treatment of pain, stress, anxiety, depression, addictions, and many other disorders. We could add that paying attention to the real present, not the virtual present of the Internet and its distractions, could also enhance our spiritual lives. To achieve any measure of success with the digital challenges facing us in our future, we need to be disciplined in how we safeguard our Godspace. This means being mindful of, and present in, "the moment" with God.

Practicing mindfulness is learning to slow down, to do one activity at a time, and bring your full awareness to both the activity at hand and to your inner experience, to hear more and to feel more. This is known as *centering*. It helps you focus and will help you to find balance when you return to your real life. Mindfulness is also what Jesus was speaking about in Matthew 6:34, when he said, "Therefore do not worry about tomorrow, for tomorrow will worry about itself. Each day has enough trouble of its own." Jesus was teaching us to be mindful of the present presence of our real life in Christ. What we really need is less information and more application. No app in the smartest cell phone can do this for you.

Journaling

Another extremely helpful tool in helping us to master the digital invasion is journaling. It is a great aid to help us control our thoughts. The practice of journaling is highly beneficial, because when we put pen to paper, the process of writing down on paper actually consolidates the associated memory and adds clarity to what we are thinking. If you have never journaled your daily experiences, thoughts, and feelings, then try doing this for a while and see how you will become more focused. Since our eyes are each linked to both hemispheres of the brain, when we write something down, it goes immediately to the whole brain. Dr. Caroline Leaf explains the effect this way:

> It may seem a little strange at first, but this method of pouring out your thoughts encourages *both sides of the brain* to work together, integrating the two perspectives of thought—the left side of the brain looks at information from details to the big picture and the right side of the brain from the big picture to the details.[15]

Journaling helps clarify our thinking and is a way of paying attention to your life. If you write out your prayers, it will help you reflect on God's presence every day and gain insight into the ordinary and extraordinary things going on in your everyday life. It also helps you pay more attention to God. By keeping a written record of God's ways in your life, you can also see how God is working in your life over a period of time. It can help reveal how far you've come and where you're going. Review your journal entries regularly to help you see more clearly what's going on and recognize recurring desires, patterns, and life themes.

Sample Questions for Journaling

For those beginners at journaling, you may struggle to find topics to write about. These are some questions you can ask yourself to get a jump-start:

What drains me of energy?

What energizes me?

What are my stressors, struggles, and worries?

For what can I be grateful?

What would I like to change?

What is the yearning of my heart?

Where am I with God right now?

What is God doing in me?

What do I long for Jesus to do in me?

How can I become freer to be the person God wants me to be?

Before going to your Facebook, Twitter, texts, blogs, Pinterest, or emails each day, try to take some time alone and journal. Be quiet, listen to what God is saying to your heart, and then write it down. In the long run this will be much more beneficial and fruitful than most of your Internet ventures.

Creating a Sacred Space for Your Godspace

If you're serious about meeting with God, you will need to create a sacred space, a place you LOVE to spend time in. Set it up in an inviting place in your home. I (Dr. Frejd) have turned my living room into my sacred space and this is where I meet with God every morning. I have a reclining chair in the corner with comfy pillows and a table on which I keep an open Bible, inviting me to read it. In a basket I keep all my favorite devotional books, journal, pen and paper, and index cards. I designed it to be an inviting space that I look forward to going to every day. (Sometimes, more than once a day.) This is my sacred space where there are no technology distractions.

You can develop the habit of meeting daily with God and practice silence and solitude. It will take awhile for it to become a habit, so persist. A friend of mine (Dr. Hart) and former student, Pastor Rick Warren, rightly claims that it takes forty days of repetition to develop a habit. Practicing the presence of God is a skill and a habit that you must develop. You can train your mind to remember God, and then take him with you wherever you go, especially in the hectic places of your life. Look for the short times each day where you can find silence and solitude. Use the quiet morning moments when your soul is awakening and most receptive to God. If you can, claim some quiet time after the children have gone to school. Even traffic jams on the way to work can provide a few moments of inner stillness. Throughout your day, take notice of things, like a beautiful blue sky or green fields or imposing mountains that are all around you and connect you to God.

Sanctifying Our Technology

As we close this chapter and our book, we encourage you to become more aware of the presence of God in your life, especially in those times when you engage with your digital technology. It is easy to unconsciously shut off that part of your brain that connects you with God, while you are very absorbed in your digital tasks. The boundaries between our online and offline life are not very clear, nor very strong, and this makes practicing the presence of God online even more difficult, if possible at all!

If you have a Bible app on your smartphone, make an effort to read Scripture throughout your day. Don't just leave it there waiting for some crisis that forces you to call upon God. Access other apps and devotionals that you think you would utilize. You can read the Bible in many translations at OneYearBible.com, as well as a devotional by Oswald Chambers, *My Utmost for His Highest* at Utmost.org. One of our favorites is *Streams in the Desert*, along with many others, at Crosswalk.com.

While it is very convenient to access these devotional and instructive sites through the Internet, be aware of how easy it is for other distractions to creep in unnoticed, like incoming emails, messages, alerts, and phone calls. These sites are great tools, but it will require extra effort on your part to avoid being sidetracked. Remember, Facebook and our online connections can never take the place of a life lived in a full-faced relationship with God.

In closing we share these words from A. W. Tozer. He never lived to experience our digital invasion, but his words sum up what we share here so succinctly.

Retire from the world each day to some private spot, even if it be only the bedroom.

Stay in the secret place till the surrounding noises begin to fade out of your heart and a sense of God's presence envelops you.

Deliberately tune out the unpleasant sounds and come out of your closet determined not to hear them. Listen to the Inward Voice till you learn to recognize it.

Stop trying to compete with others. Give yourself to God and then be what and who you are without regard to what others think. Reduce your interests to a few.

Don't try to know what will be of no service to you.

Avoid the digest type of mind—short bits of unrelated facts: cute stories and bright sayings.

Learn to pray inwardly every moment. After a while you can do this even while you work.

Practice candor, childlike honesty, and humility.

Pray for a single eye.

Read less, but read more of what is important to your inner life.

Never let your mind remain scattered for very long.

Call home your roving thoughts.

Gaze on Christ with the eyes of your soul.

Practice spiritual concentration.[16]

A.W. Tozer

A Digital Sanctifying Prayer

This is my _____
[smartphone, laptop, iPod, iPad, Facebook, Twitter, Pinterest, or LinkedIn account, etc.] and I sanctify it for God's glory and for his good purpose. May it not become an idol that I serve but a tool that I use and steward well.

In Jesus' name I pray, Amen.

Discussion Questions

1. How has technology impacted your spiritual life and Godspace?
2. How will you create a sacred space without technology distractions where you can meet with God each day?
3. Dr. Hart shares his story of being forced to unplug because of a natural disaster. Have you experienced a forced unplugging and what did you learn from the experience?
4. Read the poem "Let God Love You" on page 199 and journal what you feel as you read these words.
5. What are your ideas about journaling your thoughts to God before posting and tweeting?
6. In what ways could God sanctify your technology for his purpose?

Postscript

A Glance into the Future—
Humans versus Computers

We began this book by quoting from Aldous Huxley's 1932 book, *Brave New World*, in which he anticipates the future as a utopian new world driven by technology. Twenty-seven years later he declared, "It has happened faster than I predicted." We thought we would end this book with a few comments about where we think the future of our "not so brave" world is headed, and its implications for our children and grandchildren.

Called *technological utopianism*, a strong movement of futurists has emerged. In essence, they are optimistic about the future, believing that technology is the primary tool for carving out an ideal society. But is it all that rosy? With the gap between the haves and have-nots widening, a digital divide seems to benefit technology makers more than anyone else.

Ray Kurzweil, the pioneer of computer speech recognition, has also tried to discern the role that technology will play in our future. In his first book, *The Age of Spiritual Machines*, he presents a daring argument that with the ever-accelerating rate of technological change, computers in the future will rival humans in intelligence.[1] In a subsequent book *The Singularity Is Near*, he claims that at some time in the future, computers and humans will be combined and function as a single unit.[2] The knowledge and skills that will be embedded in our brains will be combined with the vastly greater capacity, speed,

and knowledge-sharing ability of our own computers. Speaking to a
crowd of 3,000 tech-savvy listeners, he told them:

> We are a human-machine civilization. Everybody has been enhanced
> with computer technology. They're really part of who we are. If we
> can convince people that computers have complexity of thought and
> nuance . . . we'll come to accept them as human.[3]

Such an idea wouldn't be so troubling if it was just a proposal for
a sci-fi movie. But it isn't. He is serious about his projection. Is it
possible that such a union between humans and computers can take
place at some time in the future? It seems clear that if we continue to
depend heavily on technology for educating future generations, the
merging of brain and machine is inevitable and our intelligence will
become increasingly "nonbiological." New York and New Jersey have
just announced that projections of digital avatars will be installed
as "virtual customer care representatives" in three New York–area
airports, holograms guiding flyers to their gates and providing other
logistical info. By the time our book is published, we will probably
be served at many airports by holograms simulating people who will
answer our questions and never become irritated. Will this expand
to other situations, like bank or store clerks, as customers feel more
comfortable responding to an avatar than a live person?

According to Kurzweil, there will be no clear distinction between
the human brain and the brain-machine. Neither will there be any
distinction between real reality and virtual reality. We will be able to
assume different bodies and take on a range of personae at will. He
takes it even a step further and claims that in practical terms, human
aging and illness will also be reversed; pollution will be stopped; world
hunger and poverty will be solved—like a Star Trek utopia!

But no matter how brilliant many techno-predictors are, what
strikes us is that they don't address the social, mental health, and
spiritual consequences of our brain and technology becoming amal-
gamated. They fail to identify the myriad of ways new technologies
can be used against us, nor its deeper negative impact on our minds
and spirituality. The biggest danger is that our very preoccupation
with technology can rob us of our engagement with God, nature,
and true social ties to family and friends. Overall, futurists tend to
ignore the bigger issues, such as "cyberwars," that while they would
be bloodless could still cripple and destroy the economy of a nation.

If this next generation sleeps with their cell phones and experiences phantom limb vibrations when disconnected, could they become confused about companionship? The connected generation has digitized friendships played out in texting codes and emoticons. Could this be preparing them for relationships with the inanimate? Could lower expectations for connection lead to the idea that robot companions and friendships will suffice? As Christians, now is the time for us to ask these questions, and our goal is to get the conversation going. It's too late to leave the future to the futurists—*the brave new world is here*.

Our prayer is that God will give us all the wisdom to discern between what is good and bad, and reject the bad in technology. Is it too late to stem the tide and control the direction that technology is taking? No one really knows. All we can say is if we continue to ignore the problem and allow technology to override our God-given wisdom, our offspring will face a problematic future. We were created out of community with God the Father, Son, and Holy Spirit and designed to interact and connect with real-life people in deep and meaningful ways. God uses our conversations with himself, with others, and with ourselves to transform us. The digital invasion can isolate us, and the more isolated we become, the less like God we become. We need to heed the God-given wisdom of the apostle Paul when he said:

> Don't become so well-adjusted to your culture that you fit into it without even thinking. Instead, fix your attention on God. You'll be changed from the inside out. (Rom. 12:2 Message)

Appendix A

Social Media Glossary

Parents need to know the common Internet social media sites and their related terminology. Here is a summary of the more commonly used social media sites and expressions. The terms are in alphabetical order.

avatar: A three-dimensional graphical representation of a user or the user's alter ego or character in a game or virtual world.

blog: (short for "web log") A website or part of a website where you can post regular entries of opinion pieces, news, case studies, your email newsletter archive, or anything else you want to share.

Digg: A social news website that allows members to submit and vote for articles. Articles with the most votes appear on the homepage of the site and subsequently are seen by the largest portion of the site's membership, as well as other visitors.

Facebook: The largest of the social networks. Facebook has become a favorite destination for people, businesses, and organizations to connect and share information because of its easy-to-use interface and interactive features. It's the most multimedia-friendly of the big three networks as members can post text, pictures, audio, and video. It also offers tons of applications and widgets that can make your Facebook page engaging and fun.

211

Flickr: An online photo-sharing site owned by Yahoo! Flickr lets individual users upload photos and short videos to their account and share them in photo groups based on a certain subject.

Google alert: A service offered by Google that allows users to save specific searches and receive an update whenever a new result appears on the Internet.

hashtag: A tag used on the social network Twitter as a way to annotate a message. A hashtag is a word or phrase preceded by a "#." Example: #yourhashtag. Hashtags are commonly used to show that a tweet—a Twitter message—is related to an event or conference, online or offline.

Instagram: An online photo-sharing and social networking service that enables its users to take a picture, apply a digital filter to it, and share it on a variety of social networking services.

LinkedIn: The more professional of the big three social media networks, LinkedIn lets you connect with friends, colleagues, and other people you've worked or done business with. Your profile on the network is akin to an online resume.

live-blogging (or live-tweeting): Term used to describe when someone reports "live" from an event by posting short entries to a blog during the event.

lurker: Someone on social networks who simply listens and watches but doesn't participate in conversations or the activity on the site.

mashup: Web application or digital file that contains multiple types of media drawn from preexisting sources to create a new work. Digital mashups allow individuals or businesses to create new pieces of content by combining multiple online content sources.

MySpace: One of the early social media networks. It's now mainly used by music acts and other entertainers.

news feed: Literally a feed full of news. On Facebook, the News Feed is the homepage of users' accounts where they can see all the latest updates from their friends. The news feed on Twitter is called Timeline (not to get confused with Facebook's new look, also called Timeline).

NutshellMail: A free Constant Contact service that is like a digital video recorder (DVR) for your social media networks. It will keep track of all the happenings on your Facebook, Twitter, LinkedIn, and MySpace accounts.

Pinterest: Lets you organize and share things you find on the web. People use pinboards to plan their weddings, decorate their homes, and organize their favorite recipes.

podcast: Audio programs or recordings that are syndicated online. They can be streamed or downloaded. Many are posted on and downloadable from iTunes.

Reddit: Similar to Digg. It is a social news site built upon a community of users who share and comment on stories.

Second Life: An online virtual world where users are called "residents," and they interact with each other through avatars. Residents can explore, meet other residents, socialize, participate in individual and group activities, create and trade virtual property and services with one another, and travel throughout the virtual world.

SlideShare: An online community for sharing presentations. You can upload PowerPoint, Word and PDF documents, and video to the site for sharing publicly or privately.

social bookmarks: Websites where users can store, search, organize, and share web-based content.

social media: Tools that allow the sharing of information and creation of communities through online networks of people.

social networks: Social media sites (e.g., Facebook, Twitter, LinkedIn) where people connect and interact with friends, colleagues, businesses, and organizations.

Twitter: A social media network based on micro-blog posts. Users post short updates, known as *tweets*, that can be seen by anyone.

webinar: A web-based seminar, where the presentation, lecture, or workshop is transmitted over the Internet instead of in person.

wiki: A type of user-generated website where multiple people can write and manage the content. An example is Wikipedia, an online encyclopedia.

YouTube: A video-sharing site owned by Google. Users can freely upload their own video content to the site.

Appendix B

Child's Pledge for Using the Internet Responsibly

Because I respect my parents' wisdom and loving care to protect me from any harm the Internet might cause, I promise to do the following:

1. I agree to talk to my parents so that we can set up very clear rules about when and how I can use the Internet. I agree to abide by whatever time limits they set for using the computer or any other communication device.
2. I will never give out my Internet password(s) to anyone (even my best friends) or let anyone besides family members have access to my Internet connection.
3. I will always follow the directions of my parents on how to use the Internet and will never go to any site that I know would displease them. If I am in any doubt, I will talk to my parents about it.
4. Whenever a friend or anyone else tries to get me to do something or go somewhere on the Internet that does not seem right or that scares me, I will tell my parents about it right away.
5. I will never agree to meet or have any contact whatsoever with anyone I "meet" on the Internet without my parents' permission.

6. If anyone I meet on the Internet tries to give me information or send me something that my parents would be upset about, I will tell them right away.

7. I will never give out any personal information over the Internet, like my family's address, or my telephone or cell phone number. If anyone asks for any information I will tell my parents right away.

8. I will never "bully" anyone over the Internet or anywhere else, but always try to be a good friend, even to those I do not like.

9. I will never send any sort of picture of myself or any family member to anyone who asks for it, without my parents' permission.

10. I will never download any pictures or information from the Internet, or install any software or program that could possibly harm our computer or tell others about our family, without my parents' permission.

11. If anyone tries to send me inappropriate pictures about sex or even nudity, I will report this to my parents right away.

12. I will try my best to show my parents that I can be a responsible user of the Internet, so that they can be proud of me for behaving like a responsible child.

(Parents: Feel free to add any other conditions here.)

I agree to all these pledges:

Child's signature: _____

Appendix C

Teenager's Pledge for Using the Internet Responsibly

Parents, please feel free to adapt this pledge to suit the age and sensibility of your teenager.

Because I acknowledge that the inappropriate use of the Internet can lead to serious consequences and I want my parents to see that I can deal with the challenges of the Internet, I willingly pledge the following:

1. I agree to stay in touch with my parents at all times and be open about my use of the Internet. While they agree to respect my right to privacy, I will nevertheless try to be as transparent as possible in my use of the Internet so that they can come to trust me completely.

2. My parents and I will regularly review my use of the Internet and I will respect their wisdom in responding to any cautions they may alert me to.

3. Together, we will establish rules about when and how I can use the Internet. I agree to abide by whatever time limits and

access sites they may set for using the computer or any other communication device, acknowledging that these are privileges they are granting.

4. I will never use any other computer or device to access the Internet (such as a friend's computer) without keeping them informed.

5. I will never give out my Internet password(s) to anyone (even my best friends) or let anyone besides family members have access to my Internet connection.

6. I will never agree to meet or have any contact whatsoever with anyone I "meet" on the Internet without my parents' permission.

7. If anyone I meet on the Internet tries to give me information or send me something that my parents would be upset about, I will tell them right away.

8. Realizing that identity theft is now epidemic, I will never give out any information over the Internet, like my family's address, telephone or cell phone number, or any other personal information. If anyone requests personal information about myself or any other family member, I will report it to my parents right away.

9. I will never use the Internet inappropriately, such as to "bully" or threaten anyone over the Internet or anywhere else.

10. I will never send any sort of picture of myself or any family member to anyone who asks for it, without permission.

11. Because Internet pornography addiction is now rampant, I will never access or download any pictures or information of a sexual nature that my parents would disapprove of.

12. I will not install any new software or program that could possibly harm my or our family computer without informing my parents ahead of time.

13. I will be conscious of how much time I spend on the web, phone, and other devices and will not let the use of these distractions interfere with my sleep, schoolwork, and face-to-face relationships.

14. I will try my best to show my parents that I can be a responsible user of the Internet, so that they can be proud of me for behaving responsibly.

(Parents: Add any other conditions you feel would help safeguard your teenager's Internet use.)

I agree to all these pledges:

Teen's signature: _____

Appendix D

Digital Stewardship Contract

Because I desire to have healthy use of technology and steward it well, I pledge the following:

1. I acknowledge that technology is a tool to be used to make my life simpler, to be more productive, and to embrace the many benefits.

2. I will be alert for how digital technology can become an idol to me and continue to ask for God's help to keep it in its place.

3. I will enlist an accountability partner to help keep me balanced and pure in my digital use.

4. I will not waste my real life on a virtual life but seek out ways to daily engage in real life and relationships.

5. I will incorporate face-to-face conversations and connections as much as possible and limit my virtual connections.

6. I will practice being present and in the moment with the people I encounter during my day.

7. I will have tech-free times and take a digital fast to detox as needed.

8. I will not use my digital technology as an escape from my feelings and emotions.

9. I will protect my Godspace and daily practice spiritual disciplines that cultivate my relationship with God.

10. I will not access inappropriate content through the Internet and will get Covenant Eyes if it becomes a problem.

11. I will model good digital stewardship to my family, friends, and co-workers.

I agree to all these pledges:

Your Signature:_____

Appendix E

Sample Texting Abbreviations

@TEOTD	At the end of the day	CYE	Check your email
^5	High five	DM	Direct message
2GTBT	Too good to be true	DQMOT	Don't quote me on this
2MOR/TMR	Tomorrow	DTS	Don't think so
4COL	For crying out loud	EM	Email
4EAE	Forever and ever	FWIW	For what it's worth
6Y	Sexy	Gdbi	Goodbye
AAMOF	As a matter of fact	Gr8	Great
ADAD	Another day, another dollar	I	Eye
AYS	Are you serious?	ILY	I love you
B4	Before	IMO	In my opinion
BC or B/C	Because	IRL	In real life
BF	Boyfriend	J/K	Just kidding
GF	Girlfriend	L8	Late
BFN	Bye for now	L8R	Later
BHL8	Be home late	LI	LinkedIn
BIF	Before I forget	LMBO	Laughing my butt off
BOL	Best of luck	LMK	Let me know
BR	Best regards	LOL	Laughing out loud
BTW	By the way	NP	No problem
BZ	Busy	OMG	Oh my God
C	See/sea	PLS	Please
		PPL	People

223

ROFL	Rolling on the floor laughing	TMI	Too much info
		TMOT	Trust me on this
RT	Retweet	TTYL	Talk to you later
RTHX	Thanks for the retweet	TTYS	Talk to you soon
RU/RUOK?	Are you/Are you okay?	TY	Thank you
SRY	Sorry	TNX	Thanks
TAM	Tomorrow a.m.	U	You
TAU	Thinking about you	UR	Your/You're
TBL	Text back later	W/O	Without
TCOY	Take care of yourself	WTH	What the heck
THT	Think happy thoughts	Y	Why/Yes
TMB	Tweet me back	YW	You're welcome

Appendix F

Dr. Hart's Relaxation and Christian Meditation CD

This Relaxation and Christian Meditation audio CD, with a booklet describing how to use it, is available from Dr. Hart at www.TheDigital Invasion.com.

This audio CD is designed to do four things:

1. Develop your ability to rapidly produce a deep state of muscle relaxation, called the *relaxation response.*

2. Teach you how to warm your hands as a way of switching off your stressful fight-or-flight response.

3. Teach you how to take control of your thoughts and redirect them in times of worry or high anxiety into more constructive channels and help you to sleep better.

4. Provide you with ways you can enhance your awareness of what is going on around you and overcome digital fatigue.

Appendix G

Books and Resources by Dr. Hart and Dr. Frejd

Note: All Dr. Hart's and Dr. Frejd's resources are available at www. TheDigitalInvasion.com.

Relevant Books by Dr. Hart

Sleep: It Does a Family Good: How Busy Families Can Overcome Sleep Deprivation

Thrilled to Death: How the Endless Pursuit of Pleasure Is Leaving Us Numb

The Anxiety Cure: A Proven Method for Dealing with Worry, Stress, and Panic Attacks

Adrenaline and Stress: The New Breakthrough That Helps You Overcome Stress Damage

Unmasking Male Depression: Recognizing the Root Cause to Many Problem Behaviors

A Woman's Guide to Overcoming Depression

Healing Life's Hidden Addictions

Fifteen Principles for Achieving Happiness

Habits of the Mind: Ten Exercises to Renew Your Thinking

Stress and Your Child: Know the Signs and Prevent the Harm

Stressed or Depressed? (with daughter Dr. Catherine Hart Weber)

Safe Haven Marriage: Building a Relationship You Want to Come Home To (with daughter Dr. Sharon Hart May)

Audio CDs by Dr. Hart and Dr. Frejd

Dr. Hart (see website for other CDs)

Where Has All Our Pleasure Gone?

Managing Stress and Burnout in Ministry

Stress and Your Child (2 audio CDs)

Dealing with Anxiety

Dr. Sylvia Hart Frejd

Overcoming Digital Addictions Workbook by Dr. Sylvia Hart Frejd and Dr. Archibald Hart

Scripture Meditation for Overcoming Worry, Anxiety, and Depression (audio CD)

Flourish in Real Life and Relationships Coaching, Coach Training and Women's Retreats—www.HowToFlourish.com

"Your True Love Story" Talk for women's conferences and retreats—www.HartbeatMinistries.com

Dr. Hart and Dr. Frejd are available to speak on the topic of digital health for churches, the military, universities, conferences, retreats, seminars, and workshops.

More details at www.TheDigitalInvasion.com
DrSylvia@TheDigitalInvasion.com

Notes

Introduction

1. Barna Group, *The Family and Technology Report*, 2011 Annual Report (Orange, a division of The reThink Group).

Chapter 1 A Brave New World?

1. Daniel Sieberg, *The Digital Diet* (New York: Random House, 2011), 5.
2. Gary Small and Gigi Vorgan, *iBrain: Surviving the Technological Alteration of the Modern Mind* (New York: Harper, 2009), 1.

Chapter 2 Awaken to Your Relationship with Technology

1. Zoe Fox, "Forget Generation Y: 18–34 Year Olds Are Now 'Generation C,'" *Mashable Tech*, Feb. 3, 2012, http://mashable.com/2012/02/23/generation-c/.
2. nmaston, "Worldwide Smartphone Population Tops 1 Billion," Strategy Analytics, Oct. 17, 2012, http://blogs.strategyanalytics.com/WDS/post/2012/10/17/Worldwide-Smartphone-Population-Tops-1-Billion-in-Q3-2012.aspx.
3. Barna, *Family and Technology Report*.
4. Ibid.
5. Nicole M. Radziwill, *Disconnected: Technology Addiction and the Search for Authenticity in Virtual Life* (Self-published, 2010), 3.
6. William Powers, *Hamlet's Blackberry: Building a Good Life in the Digital Age* (New York: HarperCollins, 2010), 17.
7. Judy Arnall, *Plugged-In Parenting: Connecting with the Digital Generation for Health, Safety and Love* (YouSpeak Productions, 2010), DVD.
8. Statistics from *US News and World Report*, February 2009.
9. Cynthia Belar, "Technology and Education," *Monitor on Psychology*, April 2012, 75.
10. Ibid
11. http://www.pearsonfoundation.org/literacy/emergent-literacy.html.
12. "The Cisco Connected World Technology Report," September 21, 2011.

13. Matt Richtel, "Students and Technology, Constant Companions" videos, NYTimes.com, November 20, 2010, http://www.nytimes.com/interactive/2010/11/21/technology/20101121-brain-interactive.html?ref=technology.

14. Matt Richtell, "A Silicon Valley School That Doesn't Compute," NYTimes.com, October 22, 2011, http://www.nytimes.com/2011/10/23/technology/at-waldorf-school-in-silicon-valley-technology-can-wait.html?pagewanted=all.

15. Ibid.

16. "The Art of Digital Ministry: The Good, the Bad, and the Uncertain," Carolyn Gordon, PhD, *Theology, News and Notes*. Spring 2012, 24. Fuller Theological Seminary, Pasadena, CA.

Chapter 3 The Rewiring of Our Brains

1. This quote is actually a summation by Stephen L. Carter, Yale professor of law, of Bertrand Russell's "marvelous essay on this subject." Stephen L. Carter, "Text a Little Less and Think a Little More," Opinion, *Bloomberg* View, Bloomberg.com, http://www.bloomberg.com/news/2012-03-02/text-a-little-less-and-think-a-little-more-stephen-l-carter.html.

2. Daniel G. Amen, *Change Your Brain, Change Your Life: The Breakthrough Program for Conquering Anxiety, Depression, Obsessiveness, Anger, and Impulsiveness* (New York: Three Rivers Press, 1998).

3. Small and Vorgan, *iBrain*, 21.

4. Nicholas Carr, quoted in Natasha Lomas, "Your Brain vs. Technology," Silicon.com, 2011, http://www.silicon.com/technology/hardware/2011/11/10/your-brain-vs-technology-how-our-wired-world-is-changing-the-way-we-think-39747925/5/.

5. Torkel Klingberg, *The Overflowing Brain: Information Overload and the Limits of Working Memory* (New York: Oxford University Press, 2009), 3.

6. Ibid., 70.

7. Quoted in Brenda Patoine, "Brain Development in a Hyper-Tech World," *The Dana Foundation*, August 8, 2008, http://www.dana.org/media/detail.aspx?id=13126.

8. Dr. Archibald Hart, *Thrilled to Death: How the Endless Pursuit of Pleasure Is Leaving Us Numb* (Nashville: Thomas Nelson, 2007).

9. Dr. Archibald Hart, *The Anxiety Cure* (Nashville: Thomas Nelson, 2001).

10. Klingberg, *Overflowing Brain*, 7.

11. Matt Richtell, "Digital Devices Deprive Brain of Needed Downtime," *New York Times*, August 24, 2010, B1.

12. Ibid.

13. Robert Stickgold, "Sleep, Learning, and Memory," *Healthy Sleep*, 2007, http://healthysleep.med.harvard.edu/healthy/matters/benefits-of-sleep/learning-memory.

14. Dr. Archibald Hart, *Sleep: It Does a Family Good* (Wheaton: Tyndale, 2010).

15. Small and Vorgan, *iBrain*, 117.

16. Carter, "Text a Little Less."

17. Diane Ackerman, *An Alchemy of the Mind: The Marvel and Mystery of the Brain* (New York: Scribner, 2004), 3.

Chapter 4 The Multitasking Myth

1. Earl of Chesterfield, "Letter X," *Earl of Chesterfield: Letters to His Son, Part One* (Whitefish, MT: Kessinger Publishing, 2005), 15.

2. Edward M. Hallowell, *CrazyBusy: Overstretched, Overbooked, and About to Snap! Strategies for Handling Your Fast-Paced Life* (New York: Ballantine Books, 2007), 3.

3. Christine Rosen, "The Myth of Multitasking," *New Atlantis* 20 (Spring 2008): 106.

4. Klingberg, *Overflowing Brain*, 6.

5. Melanie Moran, "Training Can Improve Multitasking Ability," Phys.org, 2009, http://phys.org/news170015185.html.

6. *Microsoft Press Computer Dictionary: The Complete Standard for Business, School, Library, and Home,* 2nd ed. (Redman, WA: Microsoft Press, 1994).

7. Aater Suleman, "What Makes Parallel Programming Hard," *Future Chips*, 2011, http://www.futurechips.org/tips-for-power-coders/parallel-programming.html.

8. Peter Bregman, "How (and Why) to Stop Multitasking," *Harvard Business Review*, May 20, 2010, http://blogs.hbr.org/bregman/2010/05/how-and-why-to-stop-multitaski.html.

9. Interview with Sherry Turkle, "Digital Nation," *Frontline*, PBS, February 2, 2010.

10. Nancy Smith Kilkenny, "Study Investigates Mental Overload in Pilots," *NASA*, November 26, 2008, http://www.nasa.gov/topics/aeronautics/features/pilot_cognition .html.

11. Jeff Atwood, "Coding Horror: Programming and Human factors," *Coding Horror*, September 2006. http://www.codinghorror.com.

12. Mark Bauerlein, *The Dumbest Generation: How the Digital Age Stupefies Young Americans and Jeopardizes Our Future (Or, Don't Trust Anyone under 30)* (New York: Penguin Group, 2008), 11.

13. Rosen, "Myth of Multitasking," 107.

14. Ibid., 107.

15. Ibid., 108.

16. Hallowell, *CrazyBusy*, 12.

17. Ibid.

Chapter 5 Relationships and Social Media

1. Janet L. Surry, "Relational Psychotherapy, Relational Mindfulness," in *Mindfulness and Psychotherapy*, eds. Christopher K. Germer, Ronald D. Siegel, and Paul R. Fulton (New York: Guilford Press, 2005), 92.

2. Ibid.

3. Jean Twenge and W. Keith Campbell, *The Narcissism Epidemic* (New York: Free Press, 2010), 10.

4. Jeff Bulla, "20 Stunning Social Media Statistics Plus Infographic," *Jeffbullas's Blog*, 2012, http://www.jeffbullas.com/2011/09/02/20-stunning-social-media-statistics/.

5. John Suler, "The Online Disinhibition Effect," *CyberPsychology and Behavior* 7 (2004): 321.

6. Sherry Turkle, *Alone Together* (New York: Basic Books, 2011), lv.

7. "2009 eHarmony Marriage Metrics Study," conducted for eHarmony by Harris Interactive, http://download.eharmony.com/pdf/Harris-09-Executive-Summary.pdf.

8. Eli J. Finkel, Paul W. Eastwick, Benjamin R. Karney, Harry T. Reis, and Susan Sprecher, "Online Dating: A Critical Analysis from the Perspective of Psychological

Science," *Association for Psychology Science*, 2012, http://www.psychologicalscience. org/index.php/publications/journals/pspi/online-dating.html.

9. Les and Leslie Parrott, "dot.com Dating: Is Online Romance for You?" *Christian Counseling Today* 19 no. 3 (2012): 4.

10. Elaine Hatfield, John T. Cacioppo, and Richard L. Rapson, *Emotional Contagion*, Studies in Emotion and Social Interaction (New York: Cambridge University Press, 1994).

11. Jesse Rice, *The Church of Facebook* (Colorado Springs: David C. Cook, 2009), 197.

12. Amy Summers, "Facebook Addiction Disorder—The 6 Symptoms of F.A.D.," *Social Times*, May 2, 2011, http://socialtimes.com/facebook-addiction-disorder-the -6-symptoms-of-f-a-d_b60403.

13. Michael Austin, "Facebook Addiction? Is Facebook Harder to Quit Than Smoking?" Ethics for Everyone, *PsychologyToday*, February 20, 2012, http://www. psychologytoday.com/blog/ethics-everyone/201202/Facebook-addiction.

14. Theresa J. Borchard, "Does the Internet Promote or Damage Marriage?" *Psych Central*, 2011, http://psychcentral.com/blog/archives/2011/03/23/does-the-internet -promote-or-damage-marriage/.

15. Lindsay Shugerman, "Percentage of married couples who cheat," Catalogs. com, http://www.catalogs.com/info/relationships/percentage-of-married-couples- who-cheat-on-each-ot.html.

16. All the names and specific details have been changed to protect identity.

17. Sharon is an expert in a form of marital therapy called "Emotion Focused Therapy." It is one of the most effective forms of marital therapy available today. She also does her therapy in an "intensive format," where a couple spends several continuous days, from 8 a.m. to 5 p.m., working through their marital problems. She is the author of two books, *Safe Haven Marriage* and *How to Argue So Your Spouse Will Listen*.

18. K. Jason Krafsky and Kelli Krafsky, *Facebook and Your Marriage* (Maple Valley, WA: Turn the Tide Resource Group, 2010), 341–42.

Chapter 6 More Serious Cyber Problems

1. Josh McDowell, "Just1ClickAway," a Josh McDowell Position Paper, 2011, 2.

2. Alexa Research, as quoted in a question-and-answer format on *TesiOnline*, http://www.tesionline.com/intl/indepth.jsp?id=335.

3. Geoff Nicholson, Alexa Research, February 14, 2009. Quoted in "Web Surfers Prefer Sex over MP3!" SharewareMusicMachine.com, March 23, 2001, http://www. hitsquad.com/smm/news/773/#body.

4. http://familysafemedia.com/pornography_statistics.html.

5. Ed Vitaliano, quoted in "Caught! Online Porn, Predators Threaten Children, Teens,"*American Family Association Journal*, January 2007. www.afajourna.org/2007/ january/0107caught.asp.

6. Dr. Philip G. Zimbardo and Nikita Duncan, "The Demise of Guys: How Video Games and Porn Are Ruining a Generation," CNN.com, May 24, 2012, http://www. cnn.com/2012/05/23/health/living-well/demise-of-guys/index.html.

7. Ibid.

8. US Department of Justice, Post Hearing Memorandum of Points and Authorities, at 1, ACLU v. Reno, 929 F. Supp. 824 (1996).

9. Mark B. Kastleman, *The Drug of the New Millennium*, 2nd ed. (Packard Technologies, 2007).

10. Ibid, chap. 3.

11. Archibald Hart, *The Sexual Man: Masculinity without Guilt* (Nashville: Thomas Nelson, 1994), 90.

12. Robert Weiss, "Is Virtual Sex Destined to Become Your New BFF?" *Psych Central*, 2012, http://blogs.psychcentral.com/sex/2012/02/is-virtual-sex-destined-to-become-your-new-bff/.

13. You can find out more at RahabsRope.com.

14. Hart, *Sexual Man*, 91.

15. Archibald Hart, Catherine Hart Weber, and Deborah Taylor, *Secrets of Eve: Understanding the Mystery of Female Sexuality* (Nashville: Word Publishing, 1998), 183.

16. Hart, *Sexual Man*, 35.

17. Amanda Lenhart, "Teens and Sexting," *Pew Internet*, December 15, 2009, http://pewinternet.org/Reports/2009/Teens-and-Sexting.aspx.

18. "Theology of Sex," An Initiative of the National Association of Evangelicals Generation Project, 2009, 19.

19. Cynthia G. Wagner, "Beating the Cyberbullies: Targets of Taunting Need Help Turning the Tables on Tormentors," *Futurist*, Sept. 1, 2008, http://www.highbeam.com/doc/1G1-183437127.html.

20. Gwenn Schurgin O'Keeffe, *Cybersafe: Protecting and Empowering Kids in the Digital World of Texting, Gaming, and Social Media* (Elk Grove Village, IL: American Academy of Pediatrics, 2010).

21. "The Effects of Gambling on Families," *Problem Gambling Institute of Ontario*, 2012, http://www.problemgambling.ca/EN/GettingHelp/Pages/TheEffectsOfGambling.aspx.

22. Luke Guttridge, "Chinese Suicide Shows Addiction Dangers: Online Life Proves Too Appealing," play.tm, June 3, 2005, http://www.play.tm/news/5928/chinese-suicide-shows-addiction-dangers/.

23. "Cause and Impact of Video Games Addiction," NDRI.com, 2010, http://ndri.com/article/cause_and_impact_of_video_games_addiction_-211.html.

24. John Gaudiosi, "Gaming Is a Top Priority for Mobile-Tech Makers," CNN.com, March 1, 2012, http://www.cnn.com/2012/02/28/tech/gaming-gadgets/mwc-mobile-games/index.html?iref=allsearch/.

25. Matthew Arrington, "Forte Strong Announces Failure to Launch Program for 18–26 Year Olds," *Yahoo News*, January 28, 2012, http://news.yahoo.com/forte-strong-announces-failure-launch-program-18-26-181221185.html.

26. Anthony Faiola, "When Escape Seems Just a Mouse-Click Away," *Washington Post*, May 27, 2006, http://www.washingtonpost.com/wp-dyn/content/article/2006/05/26/AR2006052601960.html.

27. Home Page, GamingAddiction.net, 2012, http://www.gamingaddiction.net/.

28. Kevin Roberts, *Cyber Junkie: Escape the Gaming and Internet Trap* (Center City, MN: Hazelden, 2010), 34–43.

29. Turkle, *Alone Together*, introduction.

30. Second Life, http://secondlife.com/support/downloads/.

31. Robert Lemos and Margaret Kane, "Gates: Security Is Top Priority," *CNET News*, 2002, http://news.cnet.com/2100-1001-816880.html.

32. Ibid.

Chapter 7 Overcoming Digital Addictions

1. Chelsea Clinton and James P. Steyer, "Is the Internet Hurting Children?" CNN.com, May 12, 2012, http://www.cnn.com/2012/05/21/opinion/clinton-steyer-internet-kids/index.html.

2. Dr. Archibald Hart, *Healing Life's Hidden Addictions* (Servant Publications—available as a reprint from Dr. Hart).

3. You can read more about this abuse of the brain's pleasure system in Dr. Hart's book *Thrilled to Death: How the Endless Pursuit of Pleasure Is Leaving Us Numb* (Nashville: Thomas Nelson, 2007).

4. Tony Dokoupil, "Is the Web Driving Us Mad?" *Newsweek*, July 9, 2012.

5. Kimberly S. Young, "Internet Addiction: The Emergence of a New Clinical Disorder," NetAddiction.com, 1996, http://www.netaddiction.com/articles/newdisorder.pdf.

6. Colleen Moore and John Tesh, "Moms at Risk for Internet Addiction," *Impact Publishing*, May 8, 2012, http://impactpublishing.wordpress.com/2012/05/08/moms-at-risk-for-internet-addiction/.

7. Kimberly Young, Home Page, NetAddiction.com, 2009, http://www.netaddiction.com/.

8. "Responsible Text Messaging Tips," *Common Sense Media*, Dec. 21, 2011, http://www.commonsensemedia.org/advice-for-parents/responsible-text-messaging-tips.

9. "U.S. Teen Mobile Report: Calling Yesterday, Texting Today, Using Apps Tomorrow," Nielsen.com, Oct. 14, 2010, http://blog.nielsen.com/nielsenwire/online_mobile/u-s-teen-mobile-report-calling-yesterday-texting-today-using-apps-tomorrow/.

10. K. S. Young, "Cognitive-Behavioral Therapy with Internet Addicts: Treatment Outcomes and Implications," *CyberPsychology & Behavior* 10 no. 5 (2007): 671–79.

11. N. A. Shapira, et al., "Problematic Internet Use: Proposed Classification and Diagnostic Criteria," *Depression and Anxiety* 17 (2003): 207–16.

Chapter 8 Intentional Living in a Digital World

1. *New Media Trend Watch*, November 6, 2012, http://www.newmediatrendwatch.com/markets-by-country/17-usa/123-demographics.

2. Google Official History, ComScore, date verified: 7/14/12.

3. Jeffrey Kluger, "We Never Talk Anymore: The Problem with Text Messaging," *CNN Tech*, 2012, http://www.cnn.com/2012/08/31/tech/mobile/problem-text-messaging-oms/index.html.

4. "Apple's App Store Downloads Top 25 Billion," Apple Inc. (March 5, 2012). Retrieved December 12, 2012.

5. *YouTube*, http://www.youtube.com/t/press_statistics, accessed December 12, 2012.

6. *Facebook*, http://newsroom.fb.com/Key-Facts, accessed December 12, 2012.

7. Shea Bennett, "Twitter Now Seeing 400 Million Tweets Per Day, Increased Mobile Ad Revenue, Says CEO," *All Twitter*, June 7, 2012, http://www.mediabistro.com/alltwitter/twitter-400-million-tweets_b23744, accessed December 12, 2012.

8. Study by Happiness Researchers at University of California, Riverside; University of Missouri, Columbia; and University of Texas, Austin.

9. Catherine Hart Weber, *Flourish* (Grand Rapids: Baker, 2010).

10. Ibid.

11. Ibid.

12. Doreen Dodgen-Magee, "How Is Technology Shaping Generation Y?" *Biola Magazine*, Fall 2011.

13. "What Americans Do Online: Social Media and Games Dominate Activity," Nielson.com, 2010, http://blog.nielsen.com/nielsenwire/online_mobile/what-americans-do-online-social-media-and-games-dominate-activity/.

14. http://visitsteve.com/made/selfcontrol/.

15. http://www.macupdate.com/app/mac/31289/selfcontrol.

16. Some rules are adapted from *Networketiquette*, http://www.networketiquette.net.

17. Family and Technology Report, 2011.

18. John D. Sutter, "Prominent Blogger: 'I'm Leaving the Internet for a Year,'" *CNN Tech*, May 2, 2012, http://www.cnn.com/2012/05/02/tech/web/paul-miller-quits-internet/index.html?iref=allsearch.

Chapter 9 A Parent's Digital Protection Plan

1. Michele Borba, "Plugged-in Kids Losing Quality Family Time and Empathy," MicheleBorba.com, May 20, 2012, http://www.micheleborba.com/blog/2012/05/20/is-a-plugged-in-world-reducing-childrens-empathy/.

2. American Academy of Pediatrics Committee on Public Education, "Children, Adolescents, and Television," *Pediatrics* 107 (2001): 423–26, http://pediatrics.aappublications.org/content/107/2/423.full.html.

3. "Generation M2: Media in the Lives of 8- to 18-Year-Olds," Kaiser Family Foundation Study, 2010, http://www.kff.org/entmedia/mh012010pkg.cfm.

4. Dennis Prager, "Excitement Deprives Children of Happiness," *World Net Daily Commentary*, August 7, 2007, http://www.wnd.com/2007/08/42923/.

5. Danielle Hollister, "Erma Bombeck on a Mother's Love," Bellaonline.com, 2012, http://www.bellaonline.com/articles/art19929.asp.

6. Ibid.

7. O'Keeffe, *Cybersafe*, 127.

8. Archibald Hart, *Stress and Your Child* (Dallas: Word, 1992), chap. 8.

9. Interview with Trace Embry, founder and executive director, Shepherd's Hill Academy, April 29, 2012. www.shepherdshillacademy.org.

Chapter 10 Protecting Your "Godspace"

1. Anugrah Kumar, "Apologist Josh McDowell: Internet the Greatest Threat to Christians," *Christian Post*, July 16, 2011, http://www.christianpost.com/news/internet-the-greatest-threat-to-christians-apologist-josh-mcdowell-says-52382/.

2. Timothy Keller, *Counterfeit Gods* (New York: Dutton, 2009), xvi.

3. Tim Challies, *The Next Story: Life and Faith after the Digital Explosion* (Grand Rapids: Zondervan, 2011), 116.

4. L. B. Cowman, *Streams in the Desert* (Grand Rapids: Zondervan, 1997), 96.

5. David Di Salvo, "The Brain Technology Built: An Interview with Dr. Gary Small," *Neuronarrative*, 2008, http://neuronarrative.wordpress.com/2008/12/15/the-brain-technology-built-an-interview-with-dr-gary-small/.

6. Andrew Newberg and Mark Robert Waldman, *How God Changes Your Brain* (New York: Random House, 2009), 43.

7. Dr. Curt Thompson, *Anatomy of the Soul* (Illinois: SaltRiver Publishing, 2010), 175.

8. Jennifer H. Disney, "Making Space for God," *Christianity Today*, April 23, 2001, http://www.christianitytoday.com/ct/2001/april23/4.88.html.

9. Adele Calhoun, *Spiritual Disciplines Handbook* (Downers Grove, IL: InterVarsity, 2005), 86.

10. Thomas Merton, *The Wisdom of the Desert* (New York: New Directions, 1970), 55.

11. The Bellfry in Virginia, owned by Anne Grizzle, offers Strength for the Journey Retreats and Silent Retreats where you come away and be still and listen to God's voice; visit www.bellfry.org for more information.

12. Henri Nouwen, *Making All Things New* (San Francisco: Harper & Row, 1981), 69.

13. Edwina Gately, "Let Your God Love You," *Psalms of a Laywoman* (Lanham, MD: Sheed & Ward, 1999). Reprinted by permission.

14. Blaise Pascal (French scientist, mathematician, physicist, philosopher, moralist, and writer), *Pensees* (1670, section 136).

15. Caroline Leaf, *Who Switched Off My Brain?* (Nashville: Thomas Nelson, 2009), 66.

16. A. W. Tozer, *The Best of A. W. Tozer* (Grand Rapids: Baker, 1978), 151–52.

Postscript

1. Ray Kurzweil, *The Age of Spiritual Machines: When Computers Exceed Human Intelligence* (New York: Penguin Books, 2000).

2. Ray Kurzweil, *The Singularity Is Near: When Humans Transcend Biology* (New York: Viking Adult, 2005).

3. Kurzweil, cited in Brandon Griggs, "Futurist: We'll Someday Accept Computers as Human," CNN.com, March 12, 2012, http://www.cnn.com/2012/03/12/tech/innovation/ray-kurzweil-sxsw/index.html?hpt=hp_bn8.

Dr. Archibald Hart is the author of nearly thirty books and is senior professor of psychology and dean emeritus of the school of psychology at Fuller Theological Seminary. He is well known for his ministry to churches and pastors through psychological training, education, and consultation, and he and his wife, Kathleen, are sought after by church groups around the world to speak and conduct workshops. He also serves as president of the International Network for Christian Counseling. In 2011, Dr. Hart was the recipient of the prestigious 25th Anniversary AACC Silver Award for outstanding influence and leadership in the development and advancement of Christian counseling around the world. He and his wife live in California.

Dr. Sylvia Hart Frejd is the daughter of Archibald Hart. She has a master's degree specializing in Christian counseling and an earned doctorate of ministry in leadership specializing in spiritual formation. She is also certified in Internet Addiction. Dr. Frejd has been working as a digital researcher and has published articles on the subject for *Christian Counseling Today* and for various blogs. She has also given presentations on the topic and has developed The Digital Invasion resource website. She is a Flourish in Life and Relationships Coach and coach trainer and speaks at women's conferences, seminars, and retreats around the world. She lives in Virginia with her husband, Russ, and their three digital natives.

Visit her website at www.HartbeatMinistries.com.